P9-CQZ-814

Dennis Clark began his missionary career in India in 1940. It was here he learned the first lessons of this book—how local Christians and non-Christians view the foreigner.

He continues to itinerate extensively as a member of the Bible and Medical Missionary Fellowship. He also serves the David C. Cook Foundation as consultant in communications, and his travels have taken him to over fifty nations, including the USSR and East Europe. As a student of contemporary world trends, Dennis Clark continues in close touch with the thinking and action of the younger generation in North America and Asia.

the
THIRD WORLD
and
MISSION

DENNIS E. CLARK

the
THIRD WORLD
and
MISSION

with a Foreword by
PAUL S. REES

WORD BOOKS, Publisher
Waco, Texas

THE THIRD WORLD AND MISSION
Copyright © 1971 by Word, Incorporated
4800 West Waco Drive, Waco, Texas 76710

All rights reserved. No portion of
this book may be reproduced in any form
except for brief quotations in critical
articles and reviews without the written
permission of the publisher.

Quotations marked JBP are from J. B. Phillips'
The New Testament in Modern English, copyright
J. B. Phillips 1958, published by Macmillan.

Library of Congress catalog card number: 72–134942
Printed in the United States of America

(Baker & Taylor)

To my friends and colleagues in
Pakistan, India, and the other nations of Asia
from whom I have learned so much

and

To Dr. David C. Cook III,
Dr. Albert Montgomery, Rev. Robert B. Reekie,
and the staff of the David C. Cook Foundation
through whose encouragement and help
the writing of this book was made possible

46035

Contents

Foreword

The 1959 edition of Webster's *New Collegiate Dictionary* contained the following:

Spaceship—*an imaginary aircraft of the future for interplanetary travel outside the earth's atmosphere.*

Within five years the imaginary had become the real and within a decade a moon trip had become history! It's that sort of solar system in which we live and that kind of history that is being made.

What, then, of the next ten years—the dizzying '70s that have begun to enclose us? One possible answer, rooted alike in Scripture and creed, is that the Lord may come again. "He shall come again to judge the quick and the dead" is intoned by millions—too many of them heedless—every week. The Sovereign of all history, who holds past, present, and future in His shaping hand, may intervene, consummate, punish, and reward.

Although the author of this candid and lively volume is held by such a faith and such a hope, his concern in these pages is with a form of Christian responsibility that emerges powerfully whenever we recall our Master's words, *"Occupy* till I come" (Luke 19:13). Taken in its parabolic context, the clause means, "Do business for me, trade with what I have given you, *until* my return."

In any line of business it is one part of successful merchandising just to look ahead, to interpret trends, to try to get the "feel" of the future. The role of Christians, singly and collectively, is to communicate the good news of Jesus Christ. It is also to demonstrate how that good news, if taken seriously, draws men into reconciled and reconciling communities of living faith and shared concern. The living faith requires nurture and the shared concern calls for mission.

It is the conviction of Dennis Clark that, as we proceed into the enormously volatile decade on which we have entered, the faith needs renewing and the shape of the mission needs overhauling. A European by birth, a North American by residence, an Asian by missionary-career adoption, an African, Latin-American, and Anzac by travel and study, he draws generously and, on the whole, relevantly from an immense pool of experience, exposure, and reflection.

What will the reader find in the chapters that follow?

He will find *vividness*. There is episode, conversation, local color, an informed view of what technology will do *for* us and *to* us.

He will find *boldness*. The future's missionary recruits cannot trade on mediocrity. Excellence must be their bench mark, thus killing such a comment as was made by a university student in a doctoral program who said,

"I thought most missionaries were home rejects." Or, in another area, the fear is expressed that a tragic feature of missions in the '70s will be "the continuing export of domestic disputes, tensions, and cultural taboos" to parts of the world where "in most cases they are irrelevant."

He will find *documentation.* Today's typical reader soon turns off the author whose stock in trade is the sweeping generalization and the preachy platitude. Author Clark's script, steering clear of this weakness, abounds with illustrations, ties in closely with what is situational, keeps answering the question, "Wherein?"

The reader, in the fourth place, will find *honesty.* The author's Introduction, for example, is a straightforward attempt to get some of the confusion out of the climate of discussion by *defining* what he means by terms and phrases that will appear in what he has written. Even the professional theologian, who may not be entirely satisfied with the definitions, will nevertheless applaud the purpose and the intent. And when it comes to the vexed question of group relationships—those within and those without the various "councils" of churches— what is said herein is frank and fair, biblical and balanced.

Finally, the reader will find *urgency.* The change of pace in missions must more nearly approximate the change of pace in the world situation. There is a "now-ness" under God that must grip all participants in the Christian world mission. If we make no attempt to shape events, then events will take over, and mission will suffer by default. Hacking out a bush home in order to missionize among primitive peoples is so nearly a thing of the past that if we cling to this as an image, we are done for. What we need is Christian intelligence on fire, applied to the needs of rioting university students in sophisticated Tokyo. *That* is the image of tomorrow's mission, and we had better conjure with it.

We are deeply indebted to Dennis Clark for a book that toughly tackles the realities of the tough times that are upon us.

PAUL S. REES

Introduction

This book is like a multi-image film flashing long-distance shots and close-up views of the world mission scene. Its pages deal with actual situations in real places. People and places in some instances have been shifted around, but all the facts are based on personal observations from thirty years of Christian service in the Third World. Problems are faced and solutions projected for missions in the '70s.

Having lived for twenty-five years in India and Pakistan, I naturally draw on examples from that area to illustrate principles applicable to the main theme of the book—where missions are headed in the '70s. But I am not exclusively tied to Asia. Extensive travel in the Middle East, Africa, and South America has given me a wider dimension of perspective. To see the rich diversity of church life world-wide and the fascinating patterns of behavior within the basic Christian ethic is a liberating experience. My Pakistani friends would say: "You cannot remain a frog inside a well when you travel far."

The **Third World** is popularly used to refer to the independent nations of Asia, Africa, and South America who increasingly want to determine their destinies apart from the influences and pressures of the so-called great powers. The phrase is used for descriptive convenience without endorsing the political overtones often ascribed to it.

Third World churches are the churches scattered throughout these nations in all their diversity and varying degrees of strength and weakness.

The word **Christian** is used in its original biblical and etymological meaning: a disciple of Jesus Christ.

In some places the word **evangelical** is interchanged with the word *Christian,* to emphasize the concern for evangelism—the proclamation of the gospel.

Historic Christianity refers to the stream of Christians from the first century who believe in the historicity of the Scriptures. I believe that the life, teachings, death, resurrection, and ascension of Jesus Christ are historical facts and that through repentance and faith in Him as Savior and Lord we receive eternal life. I am unreservedly committed to this position and have been since becoming a Christian in Switzerland in 1933.

Theological liberal is used to describe those who do not accept as true the historical facts of Christianity as presented in the New Testament. But usage in this book of the word *liberal* in its theological context must not be confused with liberated views in reference to cultural taboos and patterns of behavior which represent the freedom Christ has given His followers.

Colonialism is used in the historical sense of the past 150 years. An extraterritorial power invades another nation, which it then administers and subjugates. Decisions for the affairs of the subjugated nation are made on its behalf by the invading rulers. Applied to church affairs it refers to churches which are still under the suzerainty of foreigners.

It is my hope and prayer that the words of this book will help bring about a fresh implementation of biblical fellowship and partnership in missions at an international level over the next decade.

chapter one

The '70s

GOODBYE, mamaji. *I'll be back for Shanti's wedding."*
Kundan Lal quickly pressed his hand in a namaste
*(greeting) to his friends and moved through Passport
Control Bombay onto the giant 747 airbus with the 450
other passengers on their way to Europe and New York.*

*Settling into his contoured sleep chair, he leafed
through* Time, *but his mind was on his fellow travelers:
a Chinese businessman—"Hong Kong," he thought, "or
Singapore"; an Indonesian student talking with two
Canadians—he heard "CUSO" (Canadian University Students Overseas) twice; an Indian girl going back to Oxford University after spending the summer at home—
she had spoken to him as they found their seats. His
father's words as they had driven out to Santa Cruz airport held fresh meaning.*

"Son, when I was your age, we had just won swaraj
*(independence). We couldn't even afford to travel by
third-class train to the village home more than once a*

year in the long holidays. All you young people are shut-tling back and forth to the West as though it were a bus journey to Nasik."

True, thought Kundan, but his father would never imagine him washing the floor in the college cafeteria to earn more pocket money to cover dates. Only one more year and his doctoral work on the control and eradica-tion of locusts would be completed. His lips moved in a subconscious "Ram, Ram" as he dozed. "God help us," he muttered. "Still a struggle for food in the year of air-bus travel." The year: 1972.

* * *

Reiko-san bowed for the ninth time to her grand-father, and with a light step joined her friend in the line-up for supersonic flight 505 to Vancouver. The jour-ney from Tokyo would take four hours, about as long as it took to drive from Kennedy Airport, New York, to Washington, in the Friday evening rush-hour traffic.

"My brother is going back to Surabja," confided Reiko to her friend.

"Surabja?" asked her friend.

"Yes, you know, Indonesia. He's got a big TV contract for the education authorities. Grandfather and father approved."

"Your grandfather is still head of the firm?"

"Oh, they say 'head of firm,'" answered Reiko-san, "but he spends a lot of money and time helping Christian TV in Indonesia. A very good man, my respected grand-father. He helps TV programs in many countries."

The SST cruised at 40,000 feet and 1,700 mph towards Vancouver. Japan and Canada had become more deeply involved with each other in business, education, and cultural exchanges. Reiko-san was an active young woman, a member of the Tokyo Christian Womens Guild, and was on the first leg of a North American speaking tour in the year 1976. She would be visiting the worship and discussion groups which had proliferated in North America and telling them of the projects Japanese Christians were backing in Brazil and other nations of Asia and Africa as well. The year: 1976.

* * *

Teacher Mazumba adjusted the knob on the side of the TV set. The image sharpened.

"Attendez! Attendez!" He clapped his hands and switched on the EVR (electronic video recordings) cartridge. Fifty teen-age students hunched forward as the camera's eye drew them into the modern tractor plant, and they followed the foreman through the manufacturing process. "As I was saying," Mazumba continued as he switched off the set, "you are to write an essay on tractor production and use in rural Congo. Any questions?"

As the class rushed out, Mazumba lifted out the EVR cartridge and walked to the library, where he picked up another for the next class.

"Alors! Teacher Mazumba," his supervisor pushed a slip into his hand. "A delegation from UNESCO is visiting us tomorrow. Take EVR cartridge 179X—you know, the eradication and control of bilharzia, WHO project of '73, produced by Telstar here in Kinshasa."

Mazumba thought of his small son who could play in the water now without fear of the dreaded bilharzia. He pulled out the cartridge for the next day's demonstration. The year: 1978.

* * *

Little imagination is needed to dream about possible developments over the next ten years in the Third World. Trends in Western nations will spill over into the independent nations of Asia, the Middle East, Africa, and Latin America. Writers in the Western world are already thinking of the implications of scientific developments in their own environment. *Target 2067*[1] looks at Canada in the next 100 years. The jumbo 747 jetliner flew to the Paris Airshow in May, 1969, and began to operate from North America late that same year. The Franco-British Concorde will become operational at twice the speed of sound in the early '70s, followed by the second-generation American SST by 1976, which may fly at 1,700 mph.

Peoples of the world will travel globally as Europeans traveled the Continent with the advent of the railway system. Tourists will erode old frontier restrictions. New ideas and fashions, like floating pollen, will travel from one nation to the other and from continent to continent. Students, professors, teachers, musicians, artists, consultants, businessmen, technicians—the list covers all areas of life—will crisscross each other's paths and communicate with each other in the trade languages of the world.

As Asia and Africa become increasingly selective in a buyers' market and manufacture their own consumer goods in increased quantities, the sense of superiority which has obsessed Western nations for so many centuries will give place to a fresh appreciation of Third World cultural values and insights.

For the tens of millions who will never earn enough to travel to other nations, the cheap media of radio, film, TV, and literature will place ideas right into their minds through ear and eye. Schoolboys in Africa will see the far side of the moon on their school TV screen. Radio shortwave reception will be vastly improved via satellite relay. Films will bring the latest events to the peoples of all nations through education usage, public cinema, or TV screening. Global telephone and telex will improve international communication so that administrative and business decisions will be made within twenty-four hours instead of through the slow process of letter writing.

Ideas will fly by two routes. The rapid world transportation systems will increase the travel of people who will carry ideas with them. The communications media will bring ideas to those who do not travel. Either way, the "noosphere,"[2] like the nervous system of an individual, will increase interaction between all nations of the world. Teilhard de Chardin speaks of the "inevitable drawing together of mankind," which he points out "is irrevocably imposed on us by the physico-chemical structure of the earth." The thoughts expressed by Teilhard and written over a period of thirty years from 1925 to 1955 are now in the realm of actuality.

In the '70s physical facilities will in fact draw mankind together as never before in history, despite the upheavals and violence that will accompany the process. We can expect in this process the proliferation of new syntheses of cultures and at the same time a fresh awareness of the diverse cultures and behavioral patterns of life among the nations of the Third World.

Another contributing factor in the total world picture is the influence of education and the changing pattern of educational requirements. In Asian and African nations the educational pattern of the '60s still reflected the Western outlook of the modern founders of the systems, who in most cases were missionaries. The pioneers of modern education transplanted the systems they knew

—systems which had evolved in the long historical development of their own nations.

In Ivory Coast, *lysée* (high school) education is recognizably related to France, with the Sorbonne, Paris, as the hopeful goal of some. So with an eye to university young Ivory Coasters learn Latin via French, although at home they speak a tribal tongue. The British mold in several nations of Asia and Africa is also recognizable. In the Philippines the American form dominates. But national educators now realize that the thousands of unemployable college graduates in India or Pakistan would have been better equipped to have had technical school preparation, a business course, or agricultural training. Expertise in political science does not necessarily fill hungry stomachs. In each nation a transition will take effect, aligning educational needs to the local situation, recasting history books, and introducing the younger generation to the world at large.

Tolerance for religious differences and an openness to syncretism in the schools and universities will pose complicated questions for believing Christians. Some will succumb to the view that all religions lead to the same goal, that no one can claim uniqueness, and that Hinduism, Buddhism, magic, or Christianity are good for differing nationalities, according to individual preference or need. The early Church faced a similar climate in its day among the sophisticates of Greece and Rome, who condescendingly offered Jesus a place in their pantheon alongside Jupiter, Venus, Apollo, and the other gods.

At the university level, Western non-Christian humanism and agnosticism have affected the minds and thinking of a number of African students among whom as "ex-Christians" it is passé to declare oneself a believing Christian. The educated class in many nations of Asia and Africa is still reacting to the colonial era and the identification of Protestant Christianity with the former colonial powers. Attitudes vary—the Muslim students of the Arab world are embittered by the continuing war with Israel, and they resent Christians as those persons somehow aligned with their enemies. In free Asia, the South Vietnam conflict and the anti-Christian regimes of North Korea, North Vietnam, and mainland China have produced an ameliorating effect on overt anti-Christian forces. But at any time the turn of events could bring about pressures on Christians in such nations as India, Pakistan, and Burma.

In the current reaction to the colonial era and the close identification of Christianity with the former Western colonial powers, we can anticipate a reaction to westernized Christianity, especially where it is openly related to foreign centers of power and influence.

At the secondary level, education provides a line of communication for Christian ideas. Millions of young people who would have remained illiterate twenty years ago will be reading by the end of the decade. Girls who for generations have remained secluded in Muslim homes or isolated in tribal villages will move by an education process into the stream of emancipated women—the wives and mothers of the '80s. They will transform the outlook of the next generation.

The ferment of young educated men and women now exposed to the latest ideas, fads, fashions, and music pulsing through the world megapolises presents the greatest challenge of the decade. The gap between their way of life and thinking and that of their parents and older leaders is so wide that in most nations youth represent a subculture little understood or penetrated by older people. In the Western world many Christian young people are by-passing church and Christian organizational structures entirely and are spontaneously associating in their own new groupings. In Asia and Africa, because of a deeper respect for age and stronger family and tribal cohesion, there is still acceptance of the authority of the elders. But tension between the younger and older generations will increase to the breaking point in many nations during the '70s.

Three more factors add to the complexities of the next decade: the conflict between affluence and poverty, industrialization and its shattering of the family, and technological developments with their depersonalizing effect.

First, the early idealism of independence has run into the hard rock of individual selfishness and corruption. As each new flag of freedom was unfurled at the United Nations, it was hoped that progress would rapidly carry the new nation into the material benefits of the twentieth century Western world. But the ancient corruptions of unredeemed life—avarice, lust, power-hunger, and self-seeking—soon showed themselves in a number of leaders. Within a decade, revolutions and coups had toppled dozens from their apparently secure seats of authority. A new national affluent elite had occupied the vacated premises and offices of the departing colonial officers, and millions remained as poor as ever. The churches had been conditioned to a docile acceptance of governmental authority. They did not know how to apply biblical truth to this kind of situation, and few Christian national voices were raised in protest. Missionaries had either signed an agreement not to touch on political issues or had been aligned with the colonial powers. As a result, little Christian instruction concerning the biblical teaching on politics was given to local Christians who were illiterate in this field. Yet because of Christian integrity, a number of Christians, especially in Africa, found themselves on call for government positions. In Asia, Christians of competence and trustworthiness found themselves in demand for certain posts. But as a whole the disparity in many nations of the Third World between the poor in city slum and village and their compatriots who live in relative luxury and wealth in the cities ferments like yeast. Already a fear clutches at the heart of the newly rich. "They will slit our throats one day," said a well-to-do Indian, wife of a government official, with three servants and two cars. Two miles away families camped under a sacking shelter and scrounged a small meal a day from heavy manual labor. She had reason to be afraid that one day the dam would burst.

Churches in Asia, Africa, and South America cannot align themselves with entrenched power or wealth. For example, in many South American nations reaction against the Roman Catholic church is a result of the backing of the *status quo* of the ruling power by the hierarchy of the church. In the Third World, Christian leaders will need to relate to the great multitudes of the poor and underprivileged as well as to speak to the relatively few rich.

Secondly, industrial developments have shattered family and tribal life over a very short period, with accompanying trauma and disintegration. The children growing up in crowded cities like Calcutta or Lagos are no longer surrounded by the milieu and long influence of family and tribal life. What has taken its place? The sorting out process will take decades, and, meanwhile, to escape from the misery of crowded tenements and airless shacks, men drink themselves senseless and leave the women to cope with the problems of little food and many obstreperous kids.

The seeds of future riots and violence have already been sown in the young teen-agers living under these conditions on the edge of affluence and luxury. In this widespread area of industrial social service where municipal and provincial governments have little taste for and lack the finances or personnel to tackle its problems, churches face a unique challenge. Here is a world far removed from air-conditioned computer consoles and jumbo jetliners. Western church politics, the preoccupations of Christian strategists at international conferences and theological debates, have little relevance in the compressed misery of tens of millions in Asia and Africa. Yet here is the twentieth century counterpart of the Gospel narratives which show Jesus among the poor, who heard Him gladly, but who were scorned by the Romans and avoided by the Pharisees.

Thirdly, technological developments in advanced Third World nations like Japan depersonalize millions upon millions. Amid the robot-like manipulation of machines and the click-clack of computers and delivery belts, men and women in white overalls will become like the slaves of science fiction. The warm human touch of Christ's servants can break the spell of industrial slavery and release those mesmerized by its demands to a life of joy and creativity.

Against the foregoing background of coming events, we can look with better perspective at Christian missions in the '70s. We can ask ourselves what major policy changes are called for, what attitudes need adjustment, and how the world of the '70s differs from the traditional mission field of the past 200 years.

chapter two

Then and Now

READY, come about!" shouts the helmsman. With timed precision the crew winches in the jib as they heel over on a new tack. It is still a long way to the finishing line, and to a landlubber they seem headed in the wrong direction; but that's how it is with wind and tide.

Missions are tacking in rough weather as the '70s open, and a wind of change is blowing. In keeping with the Great Commission, is a new tack needed? Is it time to come about, to adjust to the winds without losing way—or to abandon the race?

Many of today's missionary societies retain the strong evangelistic motivation of the nineteenth century missionary surge. The hymns and concepts of the sending churches of a century ago still pervade the atmosphere of many mission agencies today—agencies with a total of over 20,000 missionaries from North America alone.[1]

Among the underlying reasons for the persistent nineteenth century mission atmosphere is the sincere desire of the sending churches to keep the gospel undiluted and the church pure.

Two great wars between "Christian" powers, the rapid expansion of Marxism, and the penetration of previously Christian centers of learning by non-Christian humanism and anti-Christian ideologies have raised doubts in the minds of many of the Third World concerning the continuing validity of these nineteenth century missionary concepts. The world situation is radically different now.

Overt amoral paganism is featured at movie theaters in the West. The Western theater has little censorship, and modernized aspects of Sodom have attracted world-famous actors to leading roles. Orgies, wife-swapping parties, and seething campus violence have brought the darkness very, very near.

In Third World nations a Western missionary becomes very conscious of his vulnerability.

Missionary John James walked up and down platform 8 of the Calcutta railway station. He carefully avoided the sleeping forms wrapped in their dirty white sheets and smiled at the four little boys pushing to shine his shoes. He stopped again and looked at his watch. Then he noticed two youths looking at him.

"There, over there—that's him!" he heard the younger of the two say.

"Go and speak to him, Kundan! Oh, go on!" urged the other. Reluctantly, Kundan put down his book and got up from his bedding roll which was propped against the wall.

"How do you do!" Kundan had walked over to the stranger.

*"How do you do," John James replied. "Do you know
when the train leaves for Benares?"*

*"The assistant stationmaster said in another four
hours."*

*"Four hours!" echoed John James. But he would never
forget those four hours.*

*After Kundan's young brother's curiosity had been
satisfied—he had tried the transistor radio John carried,
looked at the camera, opened the cassette tape recorder
and listened to the tape—he was left with the luggage
while John and Kundan went to the restaurant. The
tension began when John said he was a missionary.*

"Why did you come here?" asked Kundan.

"God sent me."

*"But why here? Why not New York or Chicago?" John
discovered that Kundan had been a student in the
United States.*

*"Listen!" said Kundan emphatically. "You Westerners
think we are all heathen in darkness, don't you? Wasn't
that the hymn on the cassette?"*

*John couldn't explain that the hymn wasn't meant to
be played in India, and that he only carried it in memory
of his commissioning meeting a month ago. It seemed
more appropriate in the First Evangelical Church of his
hometown than here.*

> *Far, far away, in heathen darkness dwelling,*
> *Millions of souls forever may be lost.*

*Kundan continued, "I wrote those words in my note-
book when I was taken to church by a student friend in
Boston. Have you ever seen anything here in Calcutta
as obnoxious as the movie ads in Times Square?"*

Clicking his knuckles, Kundan went on relentlessly.

"Didn't you Western Christians fight each other in two world wars? And what about the drug addicts? Aren't they more lost than anyone here? Then why say the heathen are far away?"

John's knotted stomach did not relax at Kundan's final question before the train steamed in. *"John, if you have an answer to our hunger and misery, fine. But first tell me what you did for the mess in your own nation before you came here."*

John remembered briefly how he had been so busy preparing for the mission field at the seminary and then visiting churches to get support that he had done nothing for the ghetto situation or, for that matter, in suburbia, before leaving.

* * *

Whatever moral superiority Western Christendom may have shown in the past does not exist now in the minds of thinkers in the Asian, African, and Latin American nations of the Third World.

It is 150 years since Reginald Heber penned the famous lines of the hymn vocalizing the sense of responsibility which motivated the churches of Western Christendom:

> From Greenland's icy mountains,
>   From India's coral strand,
> They call us to deliver
>   Their land from error's chain.

In those days missionaries from the West sailed to the remotest corners of the earth to pioneer and preach the gospel in unknown territories and return—if they were fortunate enough to survive—to tell of the triumphs of the gospel among strange peoples.

Today, violence, anarchy, and corruption in Europe and North America vie with similar events in the Third World. A professor returning to Berkeley in May, 1969, said: "I had become used to riots in Pakistan and somehow connected them with the way of life of non-Christians. It shocked me after four years' absence to go home and find there, right where I had decided to go overseas to serve Christ, an identical volatile atmosphere."

Canada faces a problem of tension and violence in Quebec. In Britain the tightest security in a lifetime for a royal personage was provided at the investiture of Prince Charles as the Prince of Wales. In nearly all the countries of the world, similar situations indicate a growing state of unrest and turmoil.

In 1970 men like Kundan know the facts, and they take comfort that the West has no superior moral stance.

Western churches also have their problems. Sectors of Protestant churches in North America have turned their energies to politics and an open espousal of lawlessness and violent revolution, despite the long tradition of the separation of church and state. Western theological liberalism is tolerated within large Protestant denominations and paid for from church funds. Biblical church discipline of those who have reverted to pagan amorality has declined to the vanishing point.

On the other hand, in the Third World vital churches are demonstrating fresh spiritual power and activity. The early morning prayer meetings in Korean churches; all-night prayer meetings and evangelistic activities of the Elim Assembly at Hyderabad, India; the street preaching and joyous guitar-led choirs of Pentecostal churches in Santiago, Chile; the powerful preaching of

31

evangelistic teams in Indonesia; the firm Christian morality of the revival movement in East Africa—these present a picture of New Testament Christianity.

The tide has changed.

The '70s are a decade in which darkness and light, churches and pagan society will coexist in all nations. We are in conditions similar to those faced by first century Christians, when churches of varying power or weakness were scattered as lights in a dark world to be witnesses to their risen and glorified Lord, Who is the Light of the World.

Yet many churches refuse to yield their fantasy. Financial giving is tied to the emotional appeal of "the poor heathen far, far away." As soon as a seasoned missionary or approved candidate wants to work only forty miles away from the sponsoring church, his support is dropped.

"It is our policy only to support missionaries overseas" is actually written in the constitution of some churches. One returned missionary stated: "We had come to the time when we needed to remain in the United States for a few years for our teen-age children, and I saw a crucial need for evangelism among foreign students, but the board said, 'We are a missionary society; you will have to resign.' "

This subconscious attitude is prevalent, and deeply ingrained, among missionary leaders, boards, and candidates. The whole machinery of home promotion, public relations, films, and speakers is almost obliged to play the tune the sponsors wish to hear.

During the '70s Christians in the sending churches of the Western world must be led from pre-colonial to post-colonial concepts and must return to the biblical pattern: "every church in the world everywhere obligated to evangelize" (Matthew 13:38, JBP). Churches now happily supporting twenty missionaries 10,000 miles away would then consider also the inner-city ghettos ten miles from their place of worship. One practical way to bring about such a change in attitude would be for missionary societies to merge and diversify. Within the decade we could shift from the geographical fixations of 150 years to a commitment to evangelism and ministry. The biblical principle of the spiritual gifts and calling of the individual rather than the distance traveled would determine whether or not that individual would become a charge on the churches (Acts 13:1–4; 16:2–3) and a member of an operating team of workers—the missionary society.

Major changes of policy could bring renewed spiritual ministry in the sending nations and a new creative trilateral partnership in Third World nations among sending churches, receiving churches, and missionary societies. Objectives over the next ten years should include:

1. A final step in the transfer of all major policy-making concerning Christian ministry in Third World nations to the nation and region concerned, in contrast to the present practice whereby many missionary organizations still plan and direct programs for other nations from their Western bases.

2. The rise and development of teams ministering the gospel and expounding the Word of God among churches in Third World nations in which nationals would lead and direct the programs, with a minority of Western associates.

3. The development of consortiums to handle communications, with nationals in control but with Western agencies as active partners.

4. The consolidation and development of leadership training and research centers committed to historic Christianity and related to the needs of the region or nation, with nationals in leadership.

5. The grouping of missionary societies into working units, and a change of names to reflect their change of emphasis and diversification of operation, with a ministry in the sending nations as well as overseas.

6. A working financial partnership between the more affluent churches and those in greater need, to give the programs fiscal viability.

These objectives raise considerations of fiscal responsibilities, delegation of authority, recruitment, and administration procedures. How will all these affect the long history, traditions, and image of many mission agencies now in existence?

A question could also be raised: Can superorganizations created through merging do the job facing us? Cooperation in geographic and functional areas could not only preserve some of the benefits of diversity but help us to achieve the desired objectives.

Missions need to come about and make use of the wind of national self-consciousness. Instead of the domination of Christian work by Western societies in many significant Third World nations, there must be new changes, syntheses, and partnerships.

chapter three

Receiving Churches and Missions

EMERGENT and revitalized non-Christian religions threaten the churches of Asia like storm clouds on the horizon of the '70s, while in Africa, sunshine and bright skies suggest a decade of many open doors.

"They beat up two of our brothers and took away their tracts and literature. One died later of his injuries." A report from West Bengal, 1969.

"Christians are very fearful, and there is danger of their becoming an introverted ghetto like the other minority Christian communities in the Muslim world." Comment from West Pakistan, 1969.

"We can assign all the teachers we can get to religious education classes in the schools," report leaders in East Africa.

"Send us a French-speaking film producer so that we can accept the opportunity of TV programming," comes from Francophone Africa.

In Latin America, clouds and sunshine chase each

other across the sky. The fermenting revolutionary spirit has, if anything, emphasized the new freedom enjoyed by millions of Roman Catholics who now have access to the Bible. Kenneth S. Latourette called the period 1914–1960 "Vigor amidst Storm."[1] The name is equally applicable to churches in the Third World nations as we enter the '70s.

In addition to external pressures, Third World churches face two other interrelated problems: domestic dissension due to assumption of responsibility for their own affairs and repercussions from the influences of Western missionaries and fraternal workers.

Domestic dissensions are often tragically paraded before non-Christian magistrates, at great expense to the litigants.

"About the court case tomorrow," Munshi Prem Chand paused, *"if the pastor and his party win—not that they will, mind you—we can appeal to the Supreme Court. The control of the church buildings meanwhile will no longer be in our hands."*

The spokesman for his five clients cleared his throat: "Is there any hope the judge will let both parties use the church? We have spent a lot of money on witnesses; we could arrange a compromise."

Lawsuits, party strife, faction, and jockeying for the assets of church property have drained churches of spiritual power and evangelistic vigor.

* * *

The missionary beachhead of a hundred years ago soon consolidated into what became known as the compound. As cities have grown and real estate values increased, some mission properties are now worth millions of dollars. Some have been handed over to the national churches, but others are still run by missionaries as foreign bases on alien soil where foreign missionary families can live and rear their children in a protective cocoon of their own culture. Here the new arrival can unpack the half-dozen trunks and barrels of personal effects and foreign chattels, to be described to the locals by the ever-watchful houseboy. The soul need of exiles is fed by the concentration of automobiles, the chitchat and hum of a foreign base, but a great stumbling block to acceptance of missionary personnel by locals is created by its presence, as well as a temptation to avarice for the relatively poor local Christian colleague.

This center of missionary activity sees the comings and goings of would-be immigrants, scholarship seekers, client church leaders, and satellite workers who have learned the clichés and prayer forms to qualify as "our national worker."

The visiting foreign board members and other friends from home, the cables, mail, and magazines all point to the compound as the command post for a foreign enterprise. The social round, the discussion of servant problems, and the missionary weekly prayer meeting attended by twenty missionaries and two faithful nationals provide a busy life for those tied to the home. Over the rest we can draw a veil; but the problem is there, in 1970 in hundreds of Third World situations. As late as 1969, in a large city of Africa, at considerable expense, a complex of buildings was just being constructed which would be dominated from its inception by foreign missionary personnel.

First of all we must look at the disparity in living

standards and *modus operandi* between foreigner and local. Though it is not so great in the metropolises of the Third World, the difference is very obvious in town and rural areas. There the employer–employee relationship between foreigner and paid worker is certain to hamper close ties of the spirit. Added to these factors is racial prejudice. In India during the '40s missionaries would place the national evangelist in the servants' quarters for the night but accept the visiting missionary as a house guest. In that era, native workers (as they were then called) were rarely invited into the mission house to talk, but were dealt with outside.

In the '60s this attitude still persisted in some parts of Africa. The young new missionary was received with special honors and quickly put in charge of some department. Locals were expected to show him deference, not because of his age and experience, but because he was a white missionary. Was it any wonder that this type of foreign missionary enterprise was viewed as colonial and that deep levels of intimacy and fellowship were inhibited by the affluence of the employer and by poor employee relationship? As these attitudes continue into the '70s, further resentment and reaction is bound to erupt.

One solution to this carry-over of the colonial era would be to dismantle all foreign mission compounds as well as to break up concentrations of foreign personnel having authority over the people who are being served. At the latest, 1975 could be set as the target date to implement this action. Concentrations of foreigners and the old type mission compound would be an anachronism by the end of the '70s.

The possible exception would be pioneer base camps serving very primitive areas. Maintaining schools for missionary children to enable them to qualify for their home university entrance may also be a valid reason for a foreign enclave, and one which can be rationally explained to local leaders. But such a base should be quite distinct in its function from all other mission activity. Existing property which can be used by responsible local Christian leadership can be transferred to the legal jurisdiction of that leadership. Other property can be sold and more modest accommodation rented among the people served.

In the Incarnation we see that God Himself voluntarily accepted the restrictions and limitations of being born into a carpenter's family in Nazareth. His identification was so real that, while remaining sinless, He was welcome at the table of publicans and sinners. Close identification with the peoples served is basic: living among them in as unobtrusive a style as health permits, reducing foreign chattels to the essentials for efficiency, and, finally, breaking free from the hardened chrysalis of mission compound walls.

Client Churches Or Free?

Outside the mission circles, yet intersecting them at every point, are the receiving churches in varying stages of development. At one end of the spectrum there are those that are completely free, for example, the Baptist churches of Burma, the Pentecostal churches in Chile, and a number of churches affiliated with the Indonesian Council of Churches. In the middle are the client churches, technically autonomous, but under the influence of foreign missions or denominations, with extraterritorial controls. At the other end are churches, new and old, still under the direction of foreigners.

About Chile, Dr. John R. Kessler writes:

Many of the Methodists never realized how strongly the Chileans felt that the missionaries had tried to prevent the free expression of the Holy Spirit. Chilean Pentecostalism owes its dual character of nationalism and spirituality to the Chilean reaction against every attempt to control the expression of the Spirit according to the insights of the foreign missionaries, coupled with an exuberant desire for the Spirit to express Himself freely in the local situation. . . . The considered opinion even of those Methodists most able to appreciate the good points in the Pentecostal revival in Chile was that the movement was doomed to become a struggling sect which would probably collapse within a few years under the weight of its own divisiveness. Instead, today the Pentecostal churches outnumber all others.[2]

In Africa, Dr. David Barrett's careful research of 7,000 church groupings[3] reveals the longing of many African Christians to be themselves. Some groups, however, have overreacted in discarding Western accretions to the Christian faith and have gone beyond the point of a minimal Christian faith.

In Asia, a number of free churches, such as the Assemblies in India, are flourishing and supporting workers and programs. This development came through the ministry of Brother Bakht Singh Chabra.

It is a paradox that sending churches are urged to send and support missionaries for "the great need on the field," when the palavers and national prayer meetings reveal another picture.

"Oh, Lord," agonized one brother, "deliver us from the missionaries!"

"Oh, God," cried another, "break their pride and smash their palaces!"

Others pray more humbly: "Father, forgive them, for they know not what they do."

Western theological liberalism, like the ancient heresy of Arius, has spread to many of the faculty of the three hundred theological seminaries and training centers of the Third World. But the vast majority of church leaders and most knowledgeable Christians still maintain the historic Christianity on which their churches were founded. They would subscribe without reservation to the Apostles' Creed, and they revere the Bible as the Word of God and final authority for faith and conduct.

When Third World church leaders travel to international conferences, they soon discover that many of their opposite numbers are somehow different.

"I just stood up in Edinburgh and told them to their faces that they had lost their first love for the Lord," confided one Indian Presbyterian leader. "Why, many of them did not even believe Jesus was born of a virgin!"

Bishop Chandu Ray of Karachi, West Pakistan, who in 1969 assumed responsibility for the Coordinating Office for Asian Evangelism in Singapore, has on many occasions told his own experience as a young Hindu.

In Simla, perched 7,000 feet high in the Himalayas, I became a Christian. I had witnessed the miracle of a Christian missionary's eyesight being restored through prayer. I loved Jesus Christ. The Bible was living and real to me. Then I went to Bishops College, Calcutta, where much that I was taught destroyed my faith and first love for the Lord. It was much later, through a couple of godly women from New Zealand working as missionaries in Karachi, that I was restored to my early faith and joy in the Lord.

The divisive and disruptive effect of Western liberal theological thought continues into the '70s. If these liberals can be called the modern counterpart of the Sadducees, we have on the other hand the modern Pharisees, with their strong emphasis on separation which is just as disruptive to the growth of host churches. In fact, there is a question as to which is the greater of the two evils. Both of these streams from the West should be required to present their credentials before being given entrée to Third World churches.

"Your health documents please!" It was quite a day when the health officers of newly emerged nations checked on the documents of their former rulers at Passport Control.
"Sorry, sir, your smallpox vaccination is out of date."
"But, my dear man, there's not the slightest likelihood . . ."
"Sorry, sir, we'll have to put you in quarantine."

The innate courtesy, politeness, and accommodating character of Third World peoples, compounded by colonial repressions, and in the case of Christians, a long period of financial subservience, make it very difficult for receiving church leaders to introduce quarantine measures. But it is the only way to keep out the pox!

Paul's words to Timothy provide a biblical example of a similar situation in his day:

Some, alas, have laid these simple weapons contemptuously aside, and, as far as their faith is concerned, have run their ships on the rocks. Hymenaeus and Alexander are men of this sort, and as a matter of fact I had to expel them from the Church to teach them not to blaspheme (1 Timothy 1:19).

But steer clear of these un-Christian babblings, which in practice lead further and further away from Christian living. For their teachings are as dangerous as

blood poisoning to the body, and spread like sepsis
from a wound. Hymenaeus and Philetus are responsible
for this sort of thing, and they are men who are palpable
traitors to the truth, for they say that the resurrection
has already occurred and, of course, badly upset some
people's faith (2 Timothy 2:16–19, JBP).

*Frank Strong felt his heart pounding. His head felt
very light, with a floating sensation, as he walked from
the car to the small room near the Bible school at La
Paz.*

*"Señor Strong,"—the question demanded concentra-
tion, he must listen—"tell us how you became a Christian." The oldest of the four Bolivian Indians put the
question through the interpreter. The immense chests of
these four men reminded Frank Strong that they were
built for living 12,000 feet above sea level, and he was
not. In fact, he felt very weak.*

*"At the age of sixteen . . ." and he began the story of
his conversion, reflecting that he had not been cross-
questioned like this very often in the past twenty-five
years.*

*"Señor Strong, tell us what you believe about Jesus
Christ, his birth, and his death," another of the elders
spoke.*

*For twenty minutes the probing went on. Suddenly it
was all over. A nodding of heads, shaking of hands, and
cups of hot coffee.*

*"We would like you to speak to the students of our
Bible school, and tonight in the church," the older man
said as a smile crossed his face. Frank Strong mused,* I
thought this was what I came for!

*"It's routine, Frank," his colleague said later. "They
always check; they don't even take my word. They want
to be sure you are sound in the faith!"*

Missions And National Workers

In the present climate of opinion in most Third World nations, is it credible to imagine nationals serving within the structure of Western missionary societies?

"Hello! Sage Britannia (puppy dog of the British)!" said one Pakistani Muslim as he spat on the ground. "How much do you get paid for your job, uh?"

"He'll always side with the missionaries," commented one pastor to the other as they watched the "national worker" drive off with the missionary in his car.

The national staff member of a foreign-controlled mission faces serious problems. Financed and directed by a society heavily dominated by Westerners and whose first loyalty is to foreign supporters, he owes extraterritorial loyalties to that society. Often the result of this situation is his alienation from local people. There are of course, always exceptions, but they are few. Missionary societies related to receiving churches do not face the same problem, because national personnel who operate from a church can do so in a more independent and dignified manner than can employees of a foreign society.

Christian leaders in Third World churches have become increasingly conscious of their responsibility to encourage evangelism beyond the borders of their nations, and to develop their own missions. Mr. Theodore Williams, an Indian, and secretary of the Indian Evangelical Mission, made this statement in his position paper given at the Singapore Congress on Evangelism, November, 1968:

It is difficult for us to think of an Asian foreign missionary. People ask, 'Why should Asian churches send missionaries to other countries? Are there not enough unevangelized people in their own lands?' The question arises out of a misunderstanding of the nature of the church and its mission. The Great Commission is equally binding on all churches. The church at Antioch sent out Paul and Barnabas even though the whole of Syria was not yet evangelized.

The vitality of teams from Indonesia, the missionary program in Bolivia sponsored by Brazilian Baptist churches, and the itinerant preaching missions in East Africa by evangelists of the Revival Movement are indicative of a pattern likely to grow in the '70s.

It seems almost too late for Western societies to recruit the national because, with very few exceptions, the stigma of being labeled a "stooge" or "puppet" reduces usefulness. The more likely pattern of development will be the strengthening of existing missionary societies in Third World nations and proliferation of others. As national workers join these groups a partnership arrangement with Western societies in certain joint projects can then be worked out.

The Western concept of "hiring and firing" overlooks the deep feeling of Christians in the Third World and can only attract "hirelings" who will flee when the wolf comes. Despite the present climate of opinion, however, there is a scramble by many societies for "key nationals," and this harasses many receiving churches, preyed on by the "servant covetor." "Thou shalt not covet thy neighbor's manservant, nor his maidservant, nor his ox, nor his ass, nor anything that is thy neighbor's" is placed alongside "Thou shalt not kill. Thou shalt not commit adultery." This principle of respect for the rights of a neighbor is clear and precise. Christian leaders visiting Third World churches are unlikely to condone murder or adultery, yet in the scramble for "key nationals" they lay themselves wide open to the charge of coveting a neighbor's servant. In the Third World, money is a factor in buying one's way into the market. One such protagonist of action wrote: "Please find the best national around, and I will pay him double his present salary."

The Evangelical Fellowship of India has in its membership requirements the following clause which must be signed by all applicants:

> *Comity:* In our relations with other Christian bodies we hold that the love of Christ and the Scriptural teaching of mutual submission constrain us:
> 1. to respect the rights of other bodies in employment of workers, and the reception of church members;
> 2. to engage in mutual consultations under dispute; and
> 3. to take no final action on a unilateral basis without the approval of the Fellowship's negotiating committee.

Larger Western denominations walk a little more carefully, but the objective of drawing nationals into their orbit is clear. Free trips to North America, scholarships, aid, grants, and the flow of foreign visitors are all part and parcel of the approach to promote, plan, and develop Christian enterprise which will be directed and influenced by foreign Christians whose first loyalty is to an alien base, not the receiving churches in a host nation.

Financial Considerations

"Where will the money come from for the work of Christ in Third World nations?" is the question many ask. Money for national churches to maintain the expensive Western superstructures which have been erected will not be readily available. But then, are most of them necessary? Have some become idols which need to be destroyed?

In the great movings of the Spirit of God in Third World nations, foreign money did not play much part anyway. In the last decade, supported by the tithes of the Christians in the area, Protestant churches in Assam have multiplied rapidly.

"That pig is for the Lord," said one hillman, pointing to a snuffling porker nearly ready for market, "and those chickens also."

"Who supports this Bible school?" asked the visitor to a thriving Bible school in the Assam hills.

"The churches," came the answer. "They give part of their income to send their young people here for training."

Finance for grass-roots work and the food and clothing necessary for dedicated evangelists is often supplied by locals if they feel responsible and are not still suffering from a paternal handout of money.

In Gujarat, India, the Christian and Missionary Alliance churches passed through a testing period when the mission decided to terminate all foreign aid at the rate of 20 percent per annum over a five-year period. There was deep resentment in the hearts and minds of many pastors, until the day when the Reverend Chavan said: "This is a challenge to us, brothers; we must depend on the Lord and not on foreigners." Through his faith and leadership, the Spirit of God broke down the bitterness and resentment, and the churches experienced widespread spiritual revival as they faced for the first time their responsibility in tithing and giving to the work of the Lord.

Looking over the bay at Concepción, Chile, the pastor pointed to a site covered by a skeleton of iron girders.

"All these churches we are showing you are earthquake-proof," the pastor said.

"Where do you get the money for these buildings?" asked the visitor.

"It is all given by local people; nothing comes from outside. We feel it is our responsibility to the Lord to provide money for our church buildings and evangelistic programs."

Finances for local church work can be supplied in nearly all cases by local people, according to their standards of income and expenditure. The introduction of foreign funds for church work has a debilitating effect and weakens local initiative.

Finances for international and regional team ministries or consortiums involved in the communications media or for central training and research centers can be donated by the more affluent churches. If monies are pooled under accredited, responsible national and regional controls, they will be neutralized and can serve the whole area and the total Christian church. Such action, in contrast to the past era of colonial controls, would be a demonstration of the unity of the Body of Christ and an expression of real partnership.

This decade may well be critical in the history of missions. Many mission leaders are perplexed and looking for fresh direction—it could come out of the storm clouds like a rainbow, from the receiving churches of Asia, Africa, and Latin America, in the flush of their first love. If leaders of those churches will step forward with new initiative and declaration of purpose in the '70s, great changes could sweep over the whole foreign missionary enterprise.

chapter four

Missions and Sending Churches

MANY church members have no interest in missions. The subject is irrelevant in their lives and therefore boring to them. And that opinion is reinforced by their reaction to many of the returning missionaries whom they have heard speak. In all fairness, however, it must be remembered that the returning missionary has been in the field so long he has lost touch with life-styles in his home country and can no longer readily relate to that society. The gulf of understanding is particularly apparent in the case of young couples in their twenties and thirties who are just becoming involved in church life.

"Did you hear Mr. Halliday is sick and won't be here this morning?" Marian remarked to the young mother on duty with her in the church nursery one Sunday morning.

"Good thing!" snapped back the young mother, trying

to quiet a bawling *five-month-old.* "*He's one of the most boring persons I've listened to. He just rambles on and on.*"

Earlier in the week, on Wednesday evening, Marian had had a similar problem with her husband, Philip.

"*Let's go,*" *Philip had said as he clicked off the TV set and watched the opening episode of* Star Trek *shrink to a tiny dot. As they made their way to the elevator he had let his resentment burst out.*

"*How did we get ourselves talked into this deal, hon?*" *he had demanded, pushing the button.* "*One of the few evenings we're alone.*"

"*Someone's got to help the missionaries.*"

"*But they're so dull, and they don't even talk our language. The last man we heard talked as if he lived in another world—didn't even communicate.*"

"*Our church supports them.*"

"*Well, it's about time we quit,*" *he said.*

"*Philip, we've got so much.*"

"*I'd rather put my money where it works.*"

"*What do you mean by that?*"

The elevator doors swung open. "*Look, hon,*" *he said as they stepped out together,* "*I just can't take this. Do you mind very much?*" *Dangling the keys, he went on.* "*Why don't you count me out tonight? Tell me all about it when you come home. Watch the bridge—traction's bad. We'll get snow tires next week.*"

Riding back up to the eighteenth floor, Philip sighed. "*Oh, well, next time I'll go.*" *He hurried back to* Star Trek. *At the door he paused.* "*Oh God—the key!*" *By the time he got back down to the parking lot, his wife was past the first traffic light, dabbing her eyes with a tissue.* "*I'll touch up my eye shadow outside the church,*" *she thought,* "*and tell them Philip is busy tonight.*"

To many Westerners the word *missions* conjures up an image of scantily clad natives among palm trees or missionaries working arduously among primitive people. For nationals of the Third World it is loaded with the emotional overtones of past history related to imperialism, colonialism, exploitation, Western supremacy and a fight for independence. Meanwhile, missionary programs in most churches remain the same as they were thirty years ago.

Church Missionary Programs

In many churches the Sunday morning service and Sunday school classes, the midweek meeting, and the small group in a home comprise the listening constituency to missionary presentations. A number of missionaries who may be excellent field personnel have lost touch with the younger generation, and it is sheer agony for them to do deputation. The antipathy is mutual. Most furloughing missionaries would greatly benefit from wide reading, contemporary film viewing, and mixing with their peers to reintegrate themselves with a nation that is four years beyond the one they left. Moreover, what a number of them really want to say is unsuitable for the morning service or the "five minutes only" slot before the pastor's sermon. Their message of concern could be much more effectively presented in a seminar where frank speaking and discussion could take place.

Philip had avoided Mr. Halliday's missionary presentation at the midweek meeting, but his imagination was triggered by a seminar which introduced the idea of regional and national communications consortiums. As a young executive, Philip knew the trends to internationalism in the business world. He had filled in at the last moment for his company at the 22nd biennial congress of the International Chamber of Commerce in Istanbul in early June, 1969, and had joined 1,800 delegates from 66 countries in the heated debate on "The Role, Rights, and Responsibilities of the International Corporation." He had even spoken with Bharat Ram of India, the new ICC chief, and had approved wholeheartedly the statement issued by the congress that, "wherever practical, international corporations should recognize the desire of countries in which they operate to participate in equity, ownership, and management."

Marian's eyes had sparkled when Philip had got to his feet and said at the seminar: "We must back these new consortiums. The world plans to involve nationals in equity ownership. We should go further, so our brothers in other nations can control their own programs. I buy this idea of partnership. This is the kind of program that'll work, and I'll put my money into it."

The Dilemma of Communication

Missionary societies and staff are constantly faced with the dilemma of what can be said about their work and what must be censored. If too much is revealed, societies fear a loss of support.

"Look, John," a senior missionary told a younger colleague on his first furlough, "this church is opposed to the World Council of Churches. Don't mention your work with those evangelical Anglicans or we'll be in trouble."

This is no new problem. Peter faced it in the first century. He ate and drank with the Gentiles until his sending church checked up on him and then, "for sheer fear of what the Jews might think," (Galatians 2:12, JBP) he withdrew from his fraternizing. Biblical record censures Peter for his dishonest attempt to cover his relationship with Gentile believers. Even Barnabas stood in such fear of the examining delegation that he joined Peter in abandoning basic principle for the sake of appearances.

Not for Export

A far more serious problem is the determination of the policy to be pursued on the field. Here the peculiar climate and outlook of the sending churches, missionary society boards, and supporting constituencies have undue influence. It is very difficult for home constituencies to understand that their criteria of judgment may not apply at all in other parts of the world and that they must refrain from making their cultural taboos and ecclesiastical disputes a factor in determining policy for the receiving nation.

For example, many evangelicals in North America continually witness the radical unbelief and permissiveness advocated by some leaders and ministers of churches related to the World Council of Churches. Indeed, there are some leaders and ministers who reject the historicity of the resurrection of Christ and repudiate such biblical morality as the Ten Commandments. They have abandoned the Christian faith. Paul's words are very applicable to such men: "They are counterfeits of the real thing, dishonest practitioners" (2 Corinthians 1:3). But to condemn all leaders and members of WCC churches and to insist on separation from them is a mistake.

In the Third World, receiving churches affiliated with the World Council of Churches or national and regional ancillaries, may be in fact, evangelical, with a dedication to Christ, a prayer life, and purity of conduct on a higher plane than the censorious church in the West. Cleavage and division among true Christians brought by home constituency pressures has weakened the work of Christ in the receiving nations. There an altogether different set of conditions and problems harasses the churches.

The missionary who has seen another picture through his overseas service faces a great dilemma. A casebook could be compiled about the lives of hundreds of men, women, and families caught in this tension. It would tell of sleepless nights, bitter tears, and return from the field for those unable to resolve the problem of whether to go along with the home board directive or to function as they know the local situation requires.

The tragedy of the '70s is the continuing export of domestic disputes, tensions, and cultural taboos to the ends of the earth. In most cases these are irrelevant to the local situation of the receiving church. In the worst instances the methods used to ensure conformity include economic boycott, defamation of character, slander, and lobbying to get an "offender" eliminated. This is very similar to the Russian doctrine of limited sovereignty—or to Rome's insistence of adherence to papal encyclical!

The biblical pattern sheds pertinent light on this problem: The receiving church in Antioch sent a delegation to the sending church at Jerusalem to deal with the problem of circumcision (Acts 15). The Antioch delegation rejected the legalism a Jerusalem delegation had attempted to impose. Neither were they ready to accept the delegation's call for separation from Gentile believers. The matter went on record in an agreement that officially left the Gentiles at Antioch free, even though the Judaizers kept up their pressures throughout the New Testament period.

Today, when and where Western-based missions insist on their home norms for Third World churches, representation needs to be made by the receiving churches to the sending churches. Such communication takes place in the large denominations through the growing number of international leader conferences where delegates are sent by the individual churches. Newer and independent churches, however, which have developed a missions program or work through faith missions, are at a disadvantage through lack of direct contact with Third World churches. They especially need to update their outlook.

The need for adequate communication is equally urgent in Europe. Among themselves European Christians are quite vocal about the unilateral way foreigners come from overseas and begin operation under their noses with little or no consultation. Yet sending churches imagine they are providing missionaries to areas devoid of evangelical life, and they have little concept of the courtesy of contacting churches in the host nation before taking any initiative.

Sending churches and mission organizations need to come to terms with some basic biblical principles of confidence and trust in the Holy Spirit's guidance and protection of the missionary they support. If that person is essentially sound in character and in biblical faith, with a deep love for Jesus Christ resulting in service overseas, why not leave him free to make decisions with his national colleagues in the milieu of church life in his host nation?

Inter-Church Ministry

Sending churches need to become receiving churches also—receiving the truth and a perspective of biblical interpretation through insight into the life of churches in other lands. Though they do not realize it, many sending churches in the West are sick—some desperately so —with the sickness of spiritual poverty living in the house of material abundance (Revelation 3:17). The time is past for thinking only of "those in darkness far, far away."

In the '70s we have moved into an era of two-way traffic. Through an increasing interchange of ministries Western churches can learn from Third World Christian speakers; the churches in the West need to listen to what men of God from other cultures have to say. Further effective reciprocal communication could take place through the hosting by Western churches of visiting Christian lay leaders, government officials, students, and church leaders arriving on an exchange basis.

Important steps in this direction have already been taken. In the United States during 1968 and 1969, COEMAR (Commission on Ecumenical Missions and Relations, United Presbyterian Church, USA) personnel worked with visiting pastors from Asia, Africa, and Latin America who teamed up with furlough missionaries to work in ghetto situations and suburbia. Urban churches facing violence and tension on their doorsteps may well turn to churches in Asia and Africa to "come over and help." In Britain a similar program can help churches serve the colored immigrants. In Germany active Christian programs among large ethnic blocs of industrial workers such as the Turks were in effect in the '60s. The pattern of increasing relationships between Western and Third World churches can be anticipated in the '70s.

Personnel Recruitment

The complex interrelatedness between sending churches, missionary societies, and receiving churches assumes new importance for Western personnel recruitment. Very few Western missionaries today have to hack out a bush home to reach primitive peoples. The majority serve in the crosscurrents we have reviewed. Maturity, experience of life, and breadth of perspective are prerequisites for church ministry.

There are other important factors, of course. Perhaps Third World youth are more easily and effectively approached by committed Western Christian youth who rub shoulders directly with them, and who present a positive, dynamic image.

"I thought most missionaries were home rejects," said one doctoral student. "They seemed to be the kids who couldn't make college and went to Bible school. They kept out of all social life, and couldn't communicate. But that was before I had met Bradley, home from Brazil. He was just great."

What had struck the student was Bradley's obvious ability, his dedication, his ability to communicate what he was doing in another culture, and his relaxed freedom to be himself in any type of society—at home, in the club, in a church, or discussing his field, which happened to be anthropology.

Western candidates for missionary work in the '70s should surely be men and women who have demonstrated their spiritual gift among their peers. All the New Testament evidence indicates a selection and support of only the best spiritually qualified persons.

The Lord Jesus selected twelve from a great number. Paul and Barnabas were probably the most qualified men at Antioch; Paul invited young men of potential leadership like Timothy to join his mobile missionary society.

Men and women with proven spiritual gifts can serve the Body of Christ in any place at any time.

With the uncertainty of tenure in any overseas assignment, the candidate should be employable in his own country, either by return to a secular job or full-time Christian ministry. The problem facing a number of missionaries is that they are not really employable at home. Is this the reason why some make haste slowly to set terminal points for handover?

Current attitudes in some Bible schools and colleges introduce serious handicaps for candidates contemplating overseas service. The student is isolated by institutional policy from the real world. One argument used in defense of this attitude is the plea of holiness, the need to protect the individual from temptation. But if candidates do not develop strength at home, how can they endure the pressures in other cultures? If rules and regulations prevent the student from mixing in the world and being exposed to the whole of life, so that Christ can be presented to pagan men and women in the West, what miracle will enable him to do this in another culture?

Students in many Bible schools and colleges (popular recruiting grounds for missions) are not permitted to attend the cinema or theater. And they do not mix with crowds of young non-Christian people who meet at popular assembly points in most cities.

One missionary candidate confided: "I don't know what to talk about. I haven't read the same books they've read or seen the movies they've seen, and I don't know much about the songs they like."

The opposite of isolation is involvement in the real world, with the ability to communicate Christ to the people who live in it.

Secular university involvement in the arts and communications media, business experience, professional life, or service in the armed forces—all provide a contemporary setting where the candidate can demonstrate his call by God to a full-time ministry of the Word and evangelism. For others, exchange scholarships and a couple of years in an overseas university will provide an introduction to new cultures.

Speaking generally, the stringent requirements of the '70s demand toughened men and women, anointed by the Holy Spirit, and schooled in the Word of God. Prolonged isolation in a Christian ghetto has such a debilitating effect on a person that it could be a disqualifying handicap. Positive qualifications for candidates offering themselves for overseas service should include a thorough knowledge of the Bible and the ability to apply it to life, demonstrated use of spiritual gift in the home environment, ability to learn a language and communicate to their peers, humility and ability to orientate to a foreign culture, and readiness to work with and *under* national Christians.

Furlough and Vacation

Missionary leave in the '70s ought to be brought into line with contemporary patterns of overseas business and professional service, and the cost calculated accordingly.

In the days of six months' travel by sailing ships, six-year terms overseas were understandable. Today, only the rich can afford the time to travel by boat. No place is much more than twenty-four hours away by air. Few secular businesses or government agencies can afford to give a year's leave to their staff.

In contrast to the long term–one year furlough pattern, a short leave every two years for the missionary to go to his homeland during the regular vacation period would provide a far more realistic plan. (The current term of service overseas by a Filipino, Indian, Congolese, or Brazilian is approximately two years.) Provision for air fares for children at school to join their parents would be included. This would keep the missionary more up to date and avoid heavy overload in his absence as well as replacement problems.

A number of missionary societies still require a four-year-or-longer term, the reason being, of course, the transportation cost. On return to his home base, after a stated rest period of about three months, the missionary commences deputation travel to inform prayer partners concerning his work and to increase financial support for return to the field. The long furlough is related to the supporting constituency's preconditioned response to the appearance of a missionary in person. In the present overall missionary pattern the absent furlough missionary has been replaced at equal cost.

Under the current plan it costs $6,000 a year to support a couple with two children in India. This includes one round trip to their homeland at the end of the fourth year. The fifth year is furlough, when a replacement couple takes over, and salaries for both couples must be paid.

The same missionary couple under the proposed substitute plan would receive a short annual vacation in the host country plus two brief trips to the homeland within a five-year term. The additional air fares would be the only cost involved. These additional air fares would be less than the cost of supporting a replacement couple for a year under the present system.

Current Plan		Proposed Substitute Plan	
Field 4 years at $6,000	$24,000	Field 5 years at $6,000	$30,000
Home furlough year		Vacation (additional	
salary	6,000	airfares)	3,370
Field replacement			
cost of another			
couple	6,000		
	$36,000		$33,370

The cash savings over a total missionary career of twenty-five years would buy a modest house per missionary.

If churches and stable fellowship groupings assume responsibility for the support of missionaries, long furloughs would not be necessary, nor the need for extensive travel in the United States to collect sufficient support.

Finance

Many Western Christians give sacrificially to the work of God overseas. On the credit side, the total sum of $300,000,000 which is given voluntarily in North America to support overseas missionary enterprise is an indication that many do care about their neighbors, that many are committed to Jesus Christ. To this sum must be added gifts for relief and special projects.

The two main issues for Western Christians to consider are putting the money where it works and evaluating the multiplicity of appeals. Where change in established giving patterns is indicated, education of the supporting constituencies is very important. The total strategy of finance needs to be explained. For example, many field jobs are better handled by nationals, with resultant great savings of cash outlay when such jobs are entrusted to them. But for lack of cash, missionaries often provide "free labor."

A literature organization asks for a missionary couple. He will spend time packing parcels and running errands. She will do the accounts. They have four children. Together with travel and education, the aggregate cost will be not less then $6,500 a year. Two Africans of spiritual gift could do the same job for $2,000 a year. The use of "free" missionary labor is often brought about because sending churches prefer to support a person they can see rather than an approved project which has no emotional appeal.

How can we determine the best use of money? Here are some guide questions:

- How would accredited national Christian leaders rate missionary personnel and programs being supported?
- Are the policies controlling the program sufficiently flexible to contribute to the established priority of the receiving churches?
- What percentage of income is applied directly to the ministry of the Word and evangelism, what percentage to institutions, and what to the promotion of the cause?

Missions can become more relevant to the modern generation of believing Western Christians and their churches or groups. In actual fact, TV, film, novels, magazines and travel have already conditioned more Westerners to life and customs in other nations than ever before. With this new, broader perspective, Christians are in a position to develop a realistic outlook toward the problems of missions and to apply biblical principles to their solution.

"It began to make sense to me," Philip told Marian as they drove home from the Seminar on Our Overseas

Responsibility, "when that guy talked in business language about a Christian consortium. Up till then I'd always thought all missionaries were out of date, living in a dream world of their own. I'm really ready to do something now."

Marion fingered the sheet of proposals that the group would decide on next week. "I don't see why we shouldn't adopt one of these projects, just as we helped the Community Chest finance the high school computerized library system," she said.

"Okay," said Philip. "I'm with you."

chapter five

Missions and Evangelism

THE '60s saw an increased concern for evangelism in the Western world. Historians will probably point to the World Congress on Evangelism, West Berlin, November, 1966, as an important watershed in global evangelism. Following the Berlin congress, regional and national congresses were convened—Africa and Asia in '68, Australia, the United States, and South America in '69, with plans for others in '70, for example, India and Canada. The initiative stemmed from Western sources, and Western finances made them possible.

The '70s could well become a decade of national evangelism with the initiative for evangelism in the Third World firmly in the hands of national leaders. National evangelists are the norm, and history is full of examples: Luther in Germany, Huss in Czechoslovakia, Bray in Cornwall, Moody in the United States.

*   *   *

Bright moonlight shone on the Urdu Bible the West Pakistani evangelist held in his left hand. Every ten minutes two strong arms reached for a lamp and pumped up the pressure. The warm dry air of the May night carried the sound of the barking dogs on the outskirts of the village. The musicians had stilled their tablas (drums) and baja (one-handed harmoniums). Over a thousand villagers crowded the open space in front of the huts, listening with rapt attention to the broad Punjabi dialect of the preacher as he drove home biblical truth using local illustrations.

"Stealing water from your neighbor's fields on a moonless night, beating your wife, buying charms from the magician, giving bribes to officials, crooked court cases . . ."

A sob broke from someone in the congregation. From another came the broken words of spontaneous prayer which quickly transformed the preaching to a prayer meeting. Conviction of sin prostrated dozens of men and women in repentance, and it was midnight before the last person slipped away to bed. The next day small groups of villagers walked miles to nearby villages to preach to their non-Christian neighbors.

An elderly Indian evangelist with a phenomenal memory stands before four thousand Muslims. His Muslim opponent in the debate waits for his turn to refute the masterly presentation of Christ's divinity, death and resurrection. The few Christians who dare to step into the meeting find their knotted stomachs relaxing. No foreigner could have emerged unscathed from such a debate. Few could have quoted so aptly from the Koran, the Bible, Al Hadith, and the Vedas to make a point. But Padre Abdul Haq, Sr., was known throughout the subcontinent for his fearless ministry to the non-

Christian. No prayer, no hymn singing, no supporting Christian crowd characterizes this approach. It is rather the modern counterpart of Paul in the Areopagus with the Athenian philosophers.

In Japan, Evangelist Honda ceremoniously bowed to the thousands who had come to hear him, and then began preaching in rapid tones. Not a foreigner was to be seen. The whole atmosphere was Japanese, including the delicate flower arrangement at the side of the platform. Young, bespectacled students listened intently to a voice familiar through radio broadcasts. They pressed on him afterwards for private discussion. Many grateful believers are in the Body of Christ today because of his ministry.

Over the bay at Concepción, Chile, the evening sun dipped low, its last rays lighting up the faces of men and women leaning out of their windows. On the street corner the six guitars fell silent as the preacher stepped forward. Small groups gathered against house walls. Young people sat on the steps with chin in hand. The musical Spanish of the preacher reached the uppermost windows, and when he had finished several followed the group to the church.

As the fifteen preaching groups converged on the church for the evening service, local people crowded in until the overflow had to stand around the doors and windows. This regular evangelistic street preaching accounts for the rapid growth of the Pentecostal churches in Chile.

Accredited national evangelists in many nations are deeply involved in their calling of proclaiming the gospel to their fellow countrymen. The methods and persons involved are as varied as the human race: lectures to students, great mass meetings, folk music groups, the witness of a Christian family, Bible study, and discussion groups. The very diversity of approach illustrates the creative working of the Holy Spirit and warns against obsession with any one technique.

Some missionaries have worked alongside national evangelists. A few have continued in the great tradition of such evangelist pioneers of a hundred years ago as Dan Crawford and Hudson Taylor. Having served their apprenticeship in a foreign language and culture, these missionaries can proclaim the gospel acceptably in a foreign land. Among the most devoted were Henry Martyn, an Islamic scholar who could have passed as a Persian, or Adoniram Judson, who so immersed himself in Buddhist culture that Burma became his country.

In the '70s all too few missionaries belong to this category of evangelists or to the apostolic tradition of Paul, whose own cultural sensitivity was strikingly illustrated in the Areopagus of Athens. On that occasion he did not quote from the Bible. There was no prayer, hymn, or benediction—only an apt quote from one of the Greeks' own poets—and yet biblical truth was so woven into his lecture that it sparked a debate, with resultant decisions (Acts 17:19–35).

Certain men have been raised up by God as evangelists to the world at large, and, with unique insight and precision, the message they proclaim in foreign cultures results in conversions. Dr. Billy Graham has vindicated his calling in this way. Such men of God transcend national and cultural differences and are God's voice to the world, His gift to the church universal.

Western evangelists in the '70s are being confronted by national consciousness which reacts against having any foreign person "come to tell us what to do." Much will be demanded of them to qualify in this changed situation for evangelism.

Two lessons should be learned from repeated comments and reactions from accredited leaders of Asia, Africa, and South America: (1) Too many foreign evangelists are coming to the major cities of the Third World, and most churches want a rest from them. (2) There is still a need for Bible teaching, and Western servants of Christ can give valuable help in this ministry.

Christian leaders in the Third World have become increasingly vocal in their reaction to the influx of foreign evangelists. What was an uncommon event in the '60s is now occurring so frequently that it has become a disturbing problem.

Complained one national leader: "Our city is the current prestige symbol for Western evangelists. We've just finished one campaign, another starts next week, and several others want us to arrange campaigns in the near future."

Many in the West feel they are "the men and women who have been called of God to evangelize the world," and they let this attitude adversely affect all their associations with the people they have come to serve. An atmosphere culturally foreign to the locals is found in many Western-sponsored evangelistic meetings, so that the gospel is heard there not as a message from the transcendent God Who calls all men everywhere to repent but as foreign propaganda. The inexperienced visitor cannot avoid Western illustrations or a westernized assumption of a background which may not exist at all in the minds of hearers. In a Pakistani village an interpreter commenting on the foreign preacher said: "When he began those illustrations about a computer, I reckoned he would take five minutes, so I put in a short message of my own. The people wouldn't have understood a thing."

Deep prejudice to the Western world is running at high tide in the early '70s. There are times in history when, however gifted a person may be, he can no longer effectively proclaim the gospel to those of another culture. A German could not have done so in Britain in 1941 nor could an Indian in Pakistan in 1967, and it will be extremely difficult for Americans to do so in the Third World in the '70s.

Still another factor making foreign evangelists generally unwelcome is the tendency of some to bypass the churches and unilaterally enter a field—including Europe—as though it were virgin territory. The biblical principle of fellowship requires evangelists to consult with local Christian leaders before action. Paul "sought out the disciples" at Tyre (Acts 2) and acceded to the pressure of local Christians not to preach or debate with an excited crowd of non-Christians at Ephesus. "The disciples would not let him" (Acts 19:30, RSV).

In Lucknow a visiting foreign evangelist coerced the local missionary against his better judgment to help him set up a mass evangelistic rally. Local Christian leaders were opposed to the program. Within a few days his rash and unwise statements resulted in a riot. He fled, and the missionary and national Christians were left to pick up the pieces. It took a couple of years for feelings to subside.

With similar incidents in other cities, it is no surprise to find national Christian leaders saying in effect: "Leave us alone please, or at least, listen to what we have to say."

On the other hand, there is widespread demand for Bible ministry to the churches, and as follow-up to evangelistic campaigns. Here is the opportunity to contribute to an area of great need: Western servants of Christ ready to help unobtrusively through exposition of Scripture, doctrinal teaching, and relating the Bible to daily life in the cultural setting.

In Indonesia tens of thousands of new Christians joined the churches in the late '60s. Many factors drew them to faith in Christ, including the ministry of national evangelistic teams. The urgent need then for Western assistance was not in starting a new mission program—as some decided to do—but for a Bible-teaching ministry within the framework of existing churches, and alongside Indonesian evangelists. Western Bible teachers ready for this approach found more openings than they could fill.

Another development during the '70s will be the increase of regional evangelistic teams comprised of nationals from the region with some Western participation. Such activity has already been demonstrated in Asia by the Asian Evangelists' Commission in which evangelists from Japan, Korea, Taiwan, the Philippines, Singapore, and India, united for specific evangelistic campaigns. They converged on Saigon in South Vietnam. They were invited to Colombo, Ceylon. They went to Indonesia. The advance work and preparation was largely assisted by a foreign adviser, Mr. Roy Robertson. The blessing of God sealed the ministry. Similar developments can be anticipated in Africa and South America, and in some instances have already taken place. Evangelism in Depth has become widely respected as a movement in South America. It involves multitudes of local church members in saturation evangelism. Leadership is in the hands of Latin Americans with the partnership of Western missionaries.

A multiplying of functional teams in which Western-ers participate in a ratio of perhaps one to five, with coordination to prevent overlapping of activity, will gradually alter the misconception that Christianity is the white man's religion. A multinational picture can re-place the colonial image of Western missions. Western missionary societies can offer personnel and finances to these free groupings of men who spend considerable time in their own national ministry, but who are pre-pared to give a proportionate allocation of time to serve their region in a team approach. The more aggressive Western societies will have a problem restraining their desire to take over, or their temptation to use the opera-tion of the team for home promotional purposes!

In the '70s we can anticipate growth in the number of evangelists from Third World nations who will also pro-claim the gospel in Western nations. The success of Oriental mysticism and music in the Western world testifies to Westerners' fascination with the Orient. The flowing robes and bare feet of the "flower children," the sitar music, the sadhu-like hair and beards, the books and magazines on yoga, Zen Buddhism, and astrology are pointers to certain voids in the hearts of Westerners. A revulsion against affluence, a hatred for the computer, a longing for nature and quietness—these could be met by an Eastern evangelist whom God may use to the Western world, hungering for Him and the mystic bliss of communion with Christ.

A visiting Third World evangelist will face difficulties, however. To remain himself and not become a copy of the Westerner, nor be caught up in a Western propaganda and public relations image, will be a challenge to his calling. Even more difficult to resist will be the temptation to become absorbed as a staff member of a Western organization where his unique contribution will be lost.

As mission organizations review their policies for the '70s a paradox is apparent. In the face of great need, very few Western missions are involved in evangelism at home. It is indeed strange, for example, that North American evangelical missions concentrate 21,000 persons plus home staff on evangelism far away and yet seem unconcerned about evangelism to fellow citizens in the United States.

Advance publicity for the USA Congress on Evangelism at Minneapolis in September, 1969, presented photographs of seventeen notable speakers, but did not include one person from the ranks of traditional evangelical missionary societies. A hundred years ago most of the speakers would have been mission leaders. The initiative for evangelism in the home nations has passed into the hands of other men.

In England one missionary society well known for its work in India and Pakistan came to a decision in the late '60s to assign one of its staff to immigrant work in Britain. This was the first step in a tradition of over 130 years of evangelism overseas to include on the total staff a missionary assigned to work at home.

The mentality of the colonial era still persists with the image of "the white man's burden." In this decade missions need to return to biblical concepts and the use of biblical terms. The word *missionary*, with its colonial implications, could well be left to rest on the history shelf and the terms *evangelist, pastor,* and *teacher* restored to their biblical dignity and importance.

The picture is not complete without passing reference

to two significant blocs of people who have been neg-
lected in the overall strategy of evangelism. Two hundred million adherents of Eastern Orthodox churches
in the Near East and Eastern Europe represent a considerable bloc of people. The new stirrings among their
youth suggest a fresh openness to the gospel. Standing
in reverence with the crowd of worshippers in Belgrade,
a smartly dressed professor united in the responses. Her
candle was burning with seventy others. Emerging into
the bright sunshine she said: "I became a true believer
a number of years ago and have a struggle as a Christian
in the university. My Marxist colleagues ridicule my
faith but respect me. But you know," she went on,
"there is something in this atmosphere of worship completely lacking in Protestant churches. I need the atmosphere of my church." Evangelism to the Orthodox
does not aim to create a replica of Western Protestant-
ism as the end result, but to introduce the new believer
to Jesus Christ as Savior and Lord.

Turkey symbolizes the abdication of responsibility
for evangelism among Muslims by very many Christians.
The bright lights of the early churches flickered out one
by one—Antioch, Ephesus, Colossae—and even the historic assembly of Nicea left no remnant. In 1970 no
churches comprised of ex-Muslim Turks worship Jesus
Christ as Lord in their mother tongue among their 34
million compatriots. The Muslims of Bosnia, Yugoslavia,
those in Bulgaria, and the twenty million of Russian
Central Asia—the Uzbeks, Tadjeks, Turkmans, Kazaks
—have never heard enough about Jesus Christ to make
an intelligent decision.

The Great Commission has never been rescinded!

chapter six

Churches and Their Training Programs

AND *what do you want to do when you are grown?"
Grandfather Elias threw some more green clover to the
buffaloes. "Mind that one," he said, restraining young
Inayat. "He butts!"*

"I want to be a preacher like uncle."

"And why a preacher?"

*"Oh, grandad, in the hot weather uncle has a machine
that makes the room cool. He has a car. He flies to
America, he . . ."*

"Now, just a minute, Inayat. Is that the real reason?"

*"Well, of course, grandad, it's a good job, better even
than Mr. Khan's. Mr. Khan's brick walls are all moldy.
Uncle has the best house in town—the one the missionary left in the riots this summer."*

The missionary had lived in good style; at least that
was how it seemed to the locals. Of course, back home
the view was that he had given up everything, and

friends often commented on his sacrificial step of faith. But his way of life was envied by locals. Some Christian job hunters qualified through seminary graduation and subsequent service to occupy the vacated mission bungalow. Inayat's uncle had finally made it. His way up had started in the Gujranwala Seminary.

Rather a contrast to the qualifications Paul outlines as a check list for ministers! He wrote: "Are they ministers of Christ? I have more claim to this title than they. . . . I have worked harder . . . served more prison sentences . . . faced death again and again. . . . I have been shipwrecked . . . have known exhaustion, pain, long vigils, hunger and thirst, doing without meals, cold and lack of clothing" (2 Corinthians 11:23–27, JBP).

Example was an integral element in the training of first century preachers, teachers and leaders. Our Lord trained the Eleven to leadership positions by choosing them to be with Him. They were like interns listening to lectures, then standing around the patients when the Great Physician skillfully diagnosed and cured the spiritual, social, and physical ills of his patients. Paul followed essentially the same pattern, and he reminded Timothy of this: "You have known intimately both what I have taught and how I have lived. My purpose and my faith are no secrets to you. You saw my endurance and patience as I met all those persecutions and difficulties . . ." (2 Timothy 3:10–11, JBP).

Western training in the past fifty years has been very heavily weighted in favor of scholarship and academic concentration, with insufficient balance of practical involvement in society. Church leaders of the Third World have now inherited many of the 350 seminaries and Bible schools requiring 'heavy subsidies. The subsidy pledged for 1965–1971 by the Theological Education

Fund alone totaled $3,402,967, of which $2,295,677 was pledged by United States bodies, $623,750 by Germany, and $198,265 by Britain.

These leaders will ask again and again: "How much of the imported teaching program is relevant and useful? What should be retained and what abandoned?"

Bold creative leadership can effect a transition to training programs relevant to local situations and true to the Word of God. This is already a major concern among national church leaders as they review five major areas of need:

1. Rural needs: In India, Pakistan, Indonesia, and many areas of Africa, millions of Christians remain in the villages. Hundreds of millions of peasants have never heard the gospel. Whereas, in Western society, urbanization increasingly concentrates populations in cities, the agricultural needs of many Third World nations are likely to remain in high priority through to the year 2000. Christian training therefore must not be so highly concentrated on sophisticated theological concepts as to neglect a Bible training for the pastors, teachers, and evangelists who will serve rural communities. This training needs to relate the Bible to life, to provide courses for farmers and their wives with advice on family planning, digging wells, increasing wheat and rice yield, exterminating pests, digging latrines, and other practical problems. Such a package training would be far more valuable than two or three years of Greek.

Bible teaching is needed to provide Christian answers to local religious views or the fear of evil spirits. Training should include hymns in the local cultural idiom, youth programs, the practical implications of how to survive on a low salary by supplementary farming, or

chicken raising. These may be more useful than a se-
mester spent discussing Arminian and Calvinistic differences.

In rural training, as in all other training, the power of
example can greatly change the outlook of the student.
One teacher, an Indian, was observed in the evenings
going for a walk in the fields. Students followed at a
distance to watch. They saw him spread his blanket on
the ground under a tree and kneel in prayer. He remained for over half an hour. This was a regular practice. His teaching on prayer in the classroom had a ring
of reality.

Another teacher, a missionary, had deliberately
chosen a mud hut which was identical to the huts in
their villages. His family sat on the floor and ate with
their fingers. When he taught he always asked questions
to force the student to apply the lesson to his own rural
situation. When this teacher took a group out for village
preaching, the students always crowded to join his team.

Our Lord combined example and practice with pre-
cept in training the Twelve. This approach comes naturally to an Indian used to the guru/chela (teacher–
disciple) relationship in the Hindu and Sikh religions.
The Western stress on academics and programing needs
modification to meet rural needs.

2. Urban areas in contrast call for an advanced training program to fit younger men to be leaders in a highly
complex community. At one end of the spectrum, national government officials, business executives, college
professors, teachers, and doctors will form part of the
church congregations. There will be young students in
the upheavals and ferment of the university world. At
the other end of the spectrum, illiterate new arrivals to
the city are looking for employment. They will come to

the pastor with the familiar refrain: "Help me find some job, sir."

Seminary and Bible school trainees for urban areas normally have a background of high school or university education upon which to build. As part of their further training, they need to study the problems of industrial society, of housing shortage, and of slum conditions and to seek the Christian answer to these problems. A young person desiring to serve Jesus Christ in the sprawling concrete jungles of the Third World cities will find himself in a complex situation where such training is essential. The conflicting ideologies, the impact of communicating media, the ferment of political discussions are the arena in which the Christian preacher will have to gain a hearing for his message.

"Today it's noon break at the 15th loom shop," Pastor Singh told the three students. The extensive cloth mills at Ahmadabad were visited weekly by the pastor and a few seminary students he brought with him. The manager was friendly, and the Bible study which they conducted in the lunch break was well attended.*

"Now we are going to the court house where five of our members are involved in a case." The young men mounted their bicycles and followed the pastor.

"Later this afternoon we're going to the film studios," Pastor Singh said as they cycled along. "I want you to meet the stars on set. One of the singers used to attend our church but . . ." The students looked at each other.

"Can we watch the shooting?"

"There may be time, but we have an appointment at the TV studios at 4:30. I am trying to get time allocation for a Christmas play," the pastor went on as he

swerved to miss a cow. "Tonight we shall divide up for the cottage meetings."

The value of practical internship as an integral element of a training program is to heighten the student's interest in Bible study. He soon discovers problems for which he must seek out the answer.

A major question in the minds of Third World church leaders is the cost of training. Who will pay the bills? Should foreign agencies continue to subsidize a Western-structured approach?

In Barcelona, Spain, evangelicals in 1969 were planning a four-year evening Bible course as an answer to the financial problems of seminary staff and students. The small minority of Protestants had found it too expensive to support a seminary and staff. By developing evening courses, students could spread their study over four years and work during the day. Lay men and women could also attend.

3. Christian education programs over the next ten years will demand a supply of teachers for all age groups in the churches. Sunday schools, as many still call them, are very weak in a number of nations.

"Why do you only have 45 children in the Sunday school when the church is packed with over 500 members?" the visitor asked the pastor.

"The thing is this," he replied. "We depended on mission schools to teach the Bible to our children, but now the government has taken over the schools and the Bible is no longer taught."

"So?" queried the visitor.

"That is the point: we shall have to do something about it now."

With the secularizing and handover of missionary schools (in certain nations of Asia), Christian education by the churches will assume importance beyond anything known in the past fifty years. The implications of such programs need to be given very careful thought so as to avoid copying Western patterns for their own sake. An example of the need for caution in this respect is a case where a Christian education diploma course was taught in a Bible school. Students began graduating and looking for jobs as directors of Christian education; very soon they discovered there were no openings at all for them, and they faced the very serious problem of looking for secular jobs to earn their living. But they were quite inadequately trained for secular employment.

In India a program was developed in the '60s to provide graded curricula slanted to the country's need. On completion of this monumental task the Christian Education Evangelical Fellowship moved into a phase of lay teacher training in many churches. In the early '70s the movement is gaining momentum with an increasing number of young people becoming involved as teachers.

4. Youth Work: Against the background of ferment and change in the Third World, wise church leaders will assess youth work as top priority. Christian youth face many problems:

- The wide cultural and mental gap between the world of urban-educated youth and that of their illiterate or up-to-fourth-grade–educated parents, and village cousins.
- An increasing fascination with modern scientific development that leaves little or no time for spiritual nurture or Christian witness.

- A reaction among educated contemporaries against westernized Christianity and therefore prejudice towards active Christians.
- An exposure to global ideas through communications media.
- Deep conflict brought about by the transition from the taboos of an older tribal generation to the modern outlook of urban youth.

Pastors do not know what to do. Parents are in deep distress, and the numbers of ex-Christian young people multiply. Given the right atmosphere and attracted by the right leaders, youthful energy can be harnessed to the great tasks of evangelism and social concern. This will alter church forms to more contemporary needs.

"Why do you go to that youth group, Samuel?" asked Prabhu Das.

"Come along and see for yourself tomorrow night. I'll pick you up on my Honda."

The two friends crowded into a small courtyard lighted by a forty-watt bulb. Seated in the corner on a reed mat was a university professor facing some thirty young students in their early twenties.

"As I was saying," repeated the professor, "you have passed through the door of knowledge. You know a little, a very little, about nuclear fission, something about vitamins and food calories. You see the disease of selfishness and corruption which is bleeding our beloved country to death. Now tonight we shall discuss two questions, and all will take part.

"Shall I have to speak?" questioned Prabhu Das in a whisper to his friend.

"*You will be jumping up yourself,*" *Samuel whispered
back. "Just wait and listen.*"

"*First question,*" *the professor went on. "What did
Jesus mean when He said 'Love your neighbor as yourself'? What practical suggestions do you have as a solution to the misery and squalor of our city, Calcutta?*"

"*Sir, sir!*" *Half a dozen hands were waving.*

"*Samuel!*"

"*Sir, it's hopeless, hopeless!*"

"*I don't agree! I don't agree!*" *More hands waved.*

Young people will be ready to learn from leaders who
can teach by questions and apply biblical truth to local
problems.

Groups of young people, associated with Brother
Bakht Singh in the '40s, led the way in replacing West-
ern-translated hymns by new Indian hymns sung to Indian tunes and accompanied by the tabla, baja and other
instruments of music. *Hymns of Zion,* as they are now
called, are today sung in thousands of churches in six
or more languages.

Drama comes naturally to many African and Asian
peoples. A youthful drama club in Mathura, India, attracted crowds at Easter as the resurrection of Christ
and His triumph over the devil was played for several
nights. Another group put on a play in New Delhi, attended by educated non-Christians.

In the Philippines, basketball teams pioneered by
Overseas Crusades have attracted many young people
and have opened a wide door for evangelism at the same
time. In Ceylon, young Christians who were startled to
see a missionary become basketball team coach to the
national team realized that sports were a key to contact their peers.

Such programs can meet the heart need of young people and involve them in Christian work. Failure at this point can lose more youth by alienation than can be gained through evangelism.

5. Advanced Training: Some men and women in the Third World will be prepared by the Holy Spirit as prophets and leaders of the churches at the national and international levels. Moses and Paul were especially qualified by their secular and religious academic background. Like them, men and women with similar qualifications will need to be ready to give up the prospects of affluence and position to serve Christ, often in relative poverty. "Moses was trained in all the wisdom of the Egyptians" (Acts 7:22). Paul had studied in the school of Gamaliel (Acts 22:3), and could quote the Greek poets. Training in business and the secular academic world is a good foundation for advanced studies in theology. Christian truth needs to be interpreted in the context of contemporary national thought and life. The leaders of the churches in the '80s will be dealing with non-Christian counterparts who in most instances will have Western degrees in addition to their own national university standing.

The time may already have come, in the early '70s, to set up graduate (and post-graduate) theological and research centers—GTRC—to serve the major regions of Asia, Africa, and South America, in preference to Western seminaries.

In the proposed GTRC projects the main objectives would be:

- The training of leaders who will present Christ to the national non-Christian so that he can think through the application of biblical truth to his own needs.

- The providing of refresher courses and leaders' retreats, with library facilities for them.
- The development of textbooks suited to regional and national training needs.
- The creative development of Christian literature as an antidote to theological liberalism and non-Christian syncretism.

"I am hoping to go to a Hong Kong study center," a Filipino graduate student said to a visitor.

"What kind of exams will you be taking?"

"I shall study for the London Bachelor of Divinity degree."

"And what has the London B.D. to do with Hong Kong or the Philippines?"

"It is recognized, you see; otherwise I shall have nothing to show for my three years' study."

The GTRC would establish its own standards suited to the local need. This may take fifteen years on the following timetable:

1. By 1975 basic B.D. training would be restricted to national and regional GTRC courses, with one center for each region.

2. By 1980 an advanced course, the equivalent of Master of Theology, would be introduced by regional faculty with the help of visiting foreign professors.

3. Normally only those who have passed through the first two stages would proceed to the West for specialized studies.

A partnership between church leaders and missionary societies could obtain these objectives.

The answer to theological liberalism and Third World syncretism is a vigorous initiative by those committed to historic Christianity and sensitive to the needs of their own people. Church leadership must recognize the increasing need for specialized ministries in the nations of the Third World, and they must examine the total spectrum in an effort to ensure that all major areas receive some attention. Specialized ministries, including film production, TV programing, radio, and literature, require special training. Church leaders should encourage young people of potential ability in these fields to secure the necessary training in them in the secular world. This generation of leaders can develop effective programs to enable Christian youth of the '70s to take up responsibility in the '80s.

Hakim clutched his father's hands as he said goodbye at Passport Control Karachi.

"Are you going very far, papa-ji?"

"Only to Beirut. I'll be back next week."

"What are you going to do in Beirut, papa?" Hakim called, as his mother took his hand.

"Meet some friends, and talk about God's work," Padre Inayat said, as he moved through the line.

Seated in the contoured chair of the Pakistani Airlines supersonic jet, Inayat thought back to the time at his grandfather's farm in the year of independence, 1947. How full of questions he had been. What he had wanted then was the good life. The Singapore Congress on Evangelism had changed all that in '68. He would never forget the passionate plea of Pak Octavianus from Indonesia:

"My Asian brothers, evangelization is our responsibility!" He manipulated his stiff arm and winced. (An angry villager had smashed his elbow with a buffalo stick. That was one type of opposition you got when preaching on the streets!)

He reached down and pulled out the agenda of the Graduate Research Center board meeting for the Mid-East region, April 15, 1981. It was going to be interesting. The Iranians had a special place in Inayat's affections. Three Coptic Egyptians would report on the Revival Movement; the new Turkish staff member was so enthusiastic about the lecture series on the Ancient Cities of Christendom. And, thought Inayat, what fellowship— and what a fine group of students!

chapter seven

Christian Leaders in the Third World

ONE by one the new flags fluttered from the white poles at the United Nations building in New York. As each new set of colors was raised, its delegation threw a party to celebrate. The high tide of colonial expansion had ebbed; the foreign rulers had gone home. By the early '60s the cry of the mid-'40s for freedom had culminated in independence for many nations of Asia and Africa. To accommodate the flow of new civil servants, embassies had to be set up in Washington and Moscow.

Many young Christian men and women who lived through the historic events of independence are now the leaders of their churches. Because of their experience in the struggles of their nations for independence they are uniquely placed to assist their churches and organizations to complete autonomy and freedom.

These men carry a heavy burden. National colleagues with innumerable problems come to them for advice and counsel and for assistance in government business.

*"Let us go and consult brother John," say two or three
with a deep local problem. In the tradition of the culture
they send a telegram and catch the train to Delhi, a
journey of one or two days.*

*In Delhi, brother John, as his friends call him, has just
returned from three hours waiting to see a government
official. In the afternoon two foreign visitors are arriving. They have cabled him: "Please arrange special meeting with all important nationals in the city at Ashok
Hotel, our expense."*

*The morning mail has brought a request from a mis-
sionary society, fearful of being ousted from India, ask-
ing him to join their local board.*

*As he sips tea, he opens a second envelope and reads:
"I have been asked to pass on to you a unanimous request from the board of the Union Seminary that you
become our chairman for the next term 1971–74. We all
sincerely hope that it will be possible for you to accept
our invitation, as we so much need your leadership and
counsel."*

The intolerable burdens some Christian leaders carry
in the Third World churches grow heavier with the
increase of travel facilities. They are caught between two
areas of need for their particular Christian capabilities:
the domestic church ministry and the growing field of
international church relationships. They are known at
home as individuals to whom to turn for advice and
counsel from the smallest of personal problems to the
weightiest of social significance; to leaders from other
nations they are known as key people upon whom to
rely for insight and communication in their national
situation.

One leader in an African state spent ten minutes listing the number of international Christian organizations which had solicited the local Christian grouping for membership and attendance at international conferences.

Having mentioned five, he said, in effect, "All will pay the travel bill. What time would there be for this country if we begin this globe-hopping?"

The words of Moses' father-in-law are very relevant: "Thou wilt surely wear away, both thou, and this people that is with thee: . . . thou art not able to perform it thyself alone. . . . thou shalt provide out of all the people able men, such as fear God . . . and place such over them. . . . And Moses chose able men" (Exodus 18:18–25, KJV).

Delegation of responsibility, involvement of Christian laymen is essential. The key to church expansion and consolidation in the first century was the appointment and recognition of local elders. It was basic to the great movements of the European reformation. In the Methodist revivals the class leaders quickly took hold of their local responsibilities. The same concept will become of crucial importance during this decade.

A very important principle at issue is the source of recognition of national leadership. Does the person hold his position of eminence because of the respect of his national colleagues or because a Western Christian group selected him as a useful person?

The church at Antioch "determined that Paul and Barnabas, and certain other of them, should go up to Jerusalem unto the apostles and elders about this question" (Acts 15:2, KJV). These men achieved their standing through recognition and appointment by their local church. The proliferation of Western-based agencies extending their interests to international concepts of operation has led to the practice of selecting key nationals through whom to work. In a number of Third World churches, as a result, two types of leaders may be found: those who are recognized by the foreign agencies, but who may not truly represent the people and those whose spiritual ministry and life have brought them to a recognized place of leadership among their own people.

"If we invite Mr. George it means we have one national speaker in the program. He seems like a good guy." The decision made in Chicago was cabled to Mr. George in Trivandrum, South India. One of the men picked up the tab of his round trip cost.

The receiving telegram clerk passed the word to some Christian leaders who met that night.

"He has isolated himself by the flashy car he bought with American money."

"There's the case of the non-existent orphanage in central India he promotes."

"His children are all in the States now, aren't they?" queries a third.

"Why don't these gentlemen consult with us here in Trivandrum?" commented the elderly chairman. "Let us pray, my brothers, let us pray."

The foreign selection of individuals and the by-passing of national and accredited leadership has caused untold complications and problems to local Christians. It will be important for evangelical Christians in the Third World to stand together in the matter of leadership and to insist on their own choices in the face of conflict with overseas initiative and contacts.

Many missionaries have been greatly humbled and spiritually enriched as they have served alongside national Christian leaders and watched the way they work. A main contrast between East and West is the deep sense of prayer burden so many carry in their heart. The Western activist has much to learn here.

"Come and pray, brother; I have a burden of prayer," the Easterner says to his Western colleague. And the two men drop to their knees for half an hour of burdened intercession for an individual.

On one occasion a physical attack on a group of Christians was halted when the leader quietly said, "We will pray now," and the whole group went to their knees. The interruption ceased in the face of earnest pleading for God's mercy on the attackers.

In another instance there seemed to be more than normal opposition to the evangelistic efforts of a devoted group of Christians. "This is a case of evil powers," the leader said. "We will call for a day of prayer and fasting." The church duly met for a whole day of prayer.

Many Indian Christians traveled hundreds of miles to a national prayer assembly at Varanasi, November 7–10, 1969, in preparation for the Congress on Evangelism the following January. Prior to this on August 15, 1969, the hundred days chain of prayer by one hundred churches commenced in the Gauhati Baptist Church, Assam. Many leaders are men of prayer.

One missionary reported a three weeks partnership with such a leader. "Late at night he was on his knees. I fell asleep under my net, but before that I could see his feet still moving to keep off the mosquitoes. I know he got into bed later, but though I was awake very early the next morning, he was already up for a long period of prayer." Such a close walk with the living Lord commands our respect, and cures the aggressive Know-It-All-Do-It-Now disease of Western Christianity.

The quality of leadership from the person who is immersed in prayer is very different from that of the status-seeker who so often is picked up—at a price—by insensitive visitors.

Orientals rebuke the Westerner by their humility and discipline. In Japan it is called "the low posture." History books will always remind us of the ascetic stance of Mr. Gandhi.

"It is not our custom, my friend," was the quiet rebuke to the Western argument for large placards and leaflets with blown-up photos of the speakers.

"Did you not read?" the words were spoken very softly. "It's in Matthew 23. You must not let people call you 'leaders'; you have only one leader, Christ. The only 'superior' among you is the one who serves the others. For every man who promotes himself will be humbled, and every man who learns to be humble will find promotion."

Humility and quietness is often mistaken for assent by Westerners. A visiting board member had arrived to help in a dispute between mission and church. Several church leaders arrived, and to the visiting board member it appeared all was going in his favor. After three hours the local leaders departed, and the missionary host saw them to the door.

As he returned to the living room the board member said: "Everything looks well wrapped up. They really bought my sales pitch."

The missionary slumped into a chair. "You didn't hear what they said as they were going out the door. 'We will be proceeding with our own program. Goodnight, brother.' That's how things are communicated here—just a quiet last word."

Cultural and tonal deafness prevents many foreign groups from hearing the clear intent of national leaders. Visitors meeting leaders for endorsement of their plans have not heard the "no" in the hesitant query and the smiling courtesies.

A main target in the '70s will be for Third World leaders to establish permanently and securely the principle that "under God and led by His Spirit, we, His people, in this nation, will determine what is best for the evangelism of our people, and how most effectively to ensure the development and strengthening of believers, so that they become fully involved as functioning members of Christ's body."

The price of leadership is very costly. The Chief Shepherd paid the price of His blood. The words of Peter to leaders, with the encouragement of the Lord's personal approval, may strengthen the many who now shoulder heavy burdens: "You should aim not at being 'little tin gods' but as examples of Christian living in the eyes of the flock committed to your charge. And then, when the Chief Shepherd reveals himself, you will receive that crown of glory which cannot fade" (1 Peter 5:3–4, JBP).

chapter eight

Christian Compassion

YOU know," Mrs. Agatha McKelvy said to the three la-
dies around the table, "I think this is one of the cutest
little restaurants in town. Just look at that view."

Before them tiny white triangles tacked to and fro
in the bay. The rain and wind had cleared the sky, and
in the distance the Golden Gate Bridge arched over the
shimmering water.

"Well, what's it to be today?" Mrs. McKelvy ran her
eye down the menu. "Crab salad—not many calories!"
The nodding heads drew in the girl for the order.

"Doris, what are you dreaming about? It's noon already."

Doris Hay snapped her attention back to the group.
She had been reflecting on the picture of a tiny little
living skeleton she had seen that morning. The child had
stared at her with big eyes from an ad in the Life magazine she had been leafing through while having her hair
done.

"*Are there really many like that?*" she had asked the girl at the beauty parlor, pointing to the skinny little form.

"*My aunt's in a relief agency called 'Compassion' or something like that. The things she tells make your skin tingle. It's worse than that from all she says.*"

"*I was just thinking of that 'Help the Needy' ad in* Life *I saw this morning, Agatha,*" Doris said. "*Two hundred dollars would be enough for medical care and food for one child for a year. The picture was terrible, terrible!*"

"*The problem is to know how much they send of what we give,*" Jessie broke in. "*The big administration boys swallow such a percentage.*"

"*Or how much gets to them of what is sent,*" said Lily. "*There's so much theft and graft.*"

Mrs. McKelvy fingered her handbag. "*One of the things that struck me on TV last night just before the eleven o'clock news was the hypocrisy of being interested in giving a few dollars for something ten thousand miles away, and doing nothing right here. Yes, right here.*" And her finger stabbed the cloth. It had been easier than she had imagined. Doris had unconsciously given the right lead, and now she would put it to them as soon as the crab was served.

"*What I want to talk to you girls about is the need for volunteers to serve in a drop-in center near the Berkeley campus.*"

"*Agatha, count me out. Why, those kids are so dirty they stink, and they might be smoking pot or something like that; I can't get mixed up in that kind of a mess.*" Doris was quite emphatic. "*In any case I'm going to get busy collecting some money for those poor starving babies.*"

One of the characteristics of many Western Christians is their almost schizophrenic capacity to assist by financial donation a humanitarian cause, while declining personal involvement with lonely and needy persons.

The classic story of the Good Samaritan is the reverse of this. He picked up the man who had been robbed and so severely beaten and, at considerable inconvenience to himself, took him to an inn where he laid out cash for his care. His parting words made it clear that he would return to check on his progress and to follow through with any further help that might be needed.

One man, commenting on church interest in missionaries, said: "We keep them like mascots or pets; they salve our conscience." Writing a check is much easier than helping derelict youth in the neighborhood. Missionary supporters will fly ten thousand miles to see the hospital or clinic they support but ignore the squalor of a colored or immigrant ghetto in their own city.

Missions involved in a multimillion-dollar aid program in other nations have, surprisingly enough, not involved themselves in the deep social problems of the sending nations. In the context of the world of the '70s a diversifying and more balanced concern for home problems may enable missions to involve younger personnel where they live before they travel to other nations.

The same principle which applies to evangelism should guide God's people in the Western world to involvement in social problems on their doorstep. In far too many cases the picture of the priest and the Levite hurrying on to some religious duty elsewhere can be seen in a contemporary setting with missions personnel. How often missions and training centers devote themselves exclusively to works of mercy far, far away, and at the same time fail to see the needs of local social programs.

This is not to deny that the physical needs of millions in Third World nations, however, do call for assistance. To the credit of all parties within the church, the social service given freely by Western missions is of a very high standard. Homes for orphans, schools for the blind and handicapped, leprosariums, hospitals, clinics, and relief agencies are respected even by antagonistic non-Christians.

"There is one thing we know about Christian orphanages," Jawaharlal Nehru once stated in a parliamentary debate. "They apply all the money they receive for the benefit of the children." During the '70s a continuing flow of assistance to the poor of the Third World will reflect the concern of many Christians to help where they can. But two important factors call for a fresh evaluation of priorities and a look at the end results.

First, the time may well have come to make a transition from a foreign directed and financed medical care and social service approach to a program that reflects the concern of national churches for their own people. One unfortunate by-product of the institutional approach by Western missionary societies has been the lack of social concern by some Christians in Third World churches. Local churches and Christians have from their birth considered institutional care an integral service of foreign churches *to them*. Few have caught the picture of *their* service to others. Further, the heavy involvement of professional missionary and paid national staff has removed the pressure which should be on each Christian to "go and do likewise."

But there are notable exceptions. A Christian doctor in

India, by choice and dedication, has foregone professional advancement and serves disfigured lepers. A nurse in Africa has declined salary increases in a government hospital in order to remain in a mission hospital where she can witness for Christ more freely. Dedicated nationals motivated by Christian compassion must be recognized and honored, of course, but we are concerned with the attitude of the average church member—the young Christian man or woman choosing a career, at the same time struggling for a minimum income on which to raise a family and care for aged parents. How can he be helped to show the compassion of Christ to a neighbor?

Some reports of Third World Christians' involvement in the urgent emergencies of their own peoples indicate an increasing social concern among average church members.

In the Bihar famine of the late '60s the Evangelical Fellowship of India took the initiative in raising and managing relief for starving villagers. From an Indian Christian constituency which was deeply involved in its own poverty there was an amazing response. With compassion as the motivation, individuals volunteered to help serve their fellow Indians in need as the light of the Gospel was seen and understood, by some for the first time.

In Indonesia, during the carnage and death following the abortive coup of 1965, the Christian attitudes of love and mercy contrasted greatly with the hatred and cruelty of the killings. Small wonder that thousands wanted to become Christians.

In the Nigerian–Biafran conflict fellow Africans from neighboring states, as well as from within the two areas, showed again and again in real and concrete forms the love of Christ for those in deep pain and misery. I interviewed two young Biafran women of Christian conviction at their camp in Ivory Coast in February, 1969. It was clear that the love and care they lavished on 300 evacuated, sick children sprang from their Christian faith, not from national duty or salary.

During the Muslim–Hindu battles for independence in 1947, the Christian community served both sides in medical teams, distribution of relief supplies, and in many emergency food stations along the routes of the fleeing thousands. The innumerable acts of compassion made a permanent impression on the refugees.

Secondly, Christians should use their very limited resources wisely. God has given basic guidelines for health and productivity, which, if followed, would enable man to manage national resources within the controlled population that can be supported. Where a continued resistance to basic biblical principles results in poverty and misery, is the answer a handout of a little food?

For example, on the admission of non-Christian Indian agronomists and agriculturalists, crop saving which could feed millions could be effected through the control of pests and vermin (rats), and wild life (monkeys). Family planning would reduce the population. Yet the deeply ingrained beliefs of Hinduism, many of which are the antithesis of Bible principles, inhibit any widespread destruction of monkeys, rats, and mice, or the control of the size of the family. "I must have a son for the funeral rites, you know."

A continual ignoring of God's law results in a final nemesis in this life on those who reject Him, as well as accountability at the final Supreme Court. Examples may be found throughout history—Egypt, the Canaan-

46035

ites, Babylon, Rome, Marxism. It is only a matter of time until all will be called upon to answer to Him.

Christ warned us not to waste our time patching old wineskins, but to fill new ones. We can best do this through a careful concentration on the redeemed community, the *ecclesia*, as a secure bridgehead in effecting change. This may be a far more fruitful effort than spreading aid over wide areas where non-Christian philosophies will swallow it like the sprinkle of rain on a desert.

There are many illustrations from history of the rapid economic development which takes place in a Christian community as it coheres and is redeemed from surrounding pagan corruption. The Armenian Christians, the Quakers, and the Mennonites are examples, as are the Christians of the Assam hills in Asia. Western Christian advisers could offer an important service in helping Third World churches over the next decade to grow in economic strength. Advice in making career choices for young people, in agricultural planning, and in business and industry could all contribute to such development. The end results can then spill over to the surrounding communities by the power of example.

Pioneer areas which open up unexpectedly call for immediate response. Following the withdrawal of the British from Aden, Yemen opened to increased medical services. A very sluggish response from Western Christians showed a regrettable state of unpreparedness. An alertness to the value of mobile units and field hospital possibilities could have enabled Christian medical missions to demonstrate compassionate concern at an opportune time.

Southern Sudan was another instance of unmet emer-

Lincoln Christian College

gency needs. With no drugs or medical services for some four million people, their plight was desperate. Bishop Elinana, writing from Uganda in May, 1969, said: "The need outside the Southern Sudan is just as acute as inside it. People are put into refugee camps. There is no attempt to get medical supplies for them; even food is a gamble."

The '70s call for the establishment of a small permanent International Christian Assistance staff to act as a clearing house for emergency situations. The mobility potential in this next decade would enable a medical team with basic supplies to be airlifted to disaster areas with further supplies to follow. Missions involved in medical work could assign personnel on a regional basis to an emergency stand-by status so that they could be called on at a moment's notice. A roster of volunteers in the United States and Canada who are ready to offer two to three months short-term service is already in operation. Such volunteers can fill in routine posts vacated by the ICA team, as well as back up the emergency teams. A fund for immediate use would put Christians right into the field of need to work alongside the churches where they exist, and in close collaboration with the Red Cross, World Health Organization and other international agencies. A careful organizational plan for each region would come into effect on receipt of a coded cable. Like the heart emergency call of a large hospital, existing personnel would be on call twenty-four hours a day.

The well-known words "God so loved the world" ring with fresh meaning as the misery, pain, and heart sob of children, men, and women cry out from earthquake debris, riots, civil war, and famine areas. God's people can now move swiftly to help them.

The only suggestion James, Cephas, and John made to Paul and Barnabas about their mission to the Gentiles was that they "should not forget the poor" (Galatians 2:10, JBP). Paul wrote much and traveled far to collect money for the famine-stricken Christians of Palestine. Compassion as a reflection of Christ's own concern for the world is a tradition of historic Christianity. The application of this principle to the '70s calls for ingenuity and fresh initiative.

chapter nine

Communications

LIVINGSTONE moved slowly through the bush, ever deeper into the unknown of Africa. Hudson Taylor broke out of the coastal cities to penetrate inland China. These men and many others opened up vast areas to the message of the gospel in the hundred or so years just past.

In the '70s there are new frontiers to which the pioneers of faith and action set forth. Man can now move beyond the gravitational pull of the earth under the sensitive guidance of electronic controls. Millions in all nations see and hear his space explorations through the advanced techniques of communications.

Ideas will penetrate to remotest towns and villages through books, film, and radio. TV will become the marketplace of the global village of the '70s; it is already a way of life for peoples in advanced nations of the Third World such as Japan. By the end of the decade other nations of Asia, Africa, and South America will follow

Japan, and TV will be a popular medium for communicating ideas to the general public, as well as for education in schools and colleges. Many millions of apathetic or non-readers who will never absorb ideas through reading can jump directly to the audio-visual media. (It was this view expressed by Marshall McLuhan which led to the coining of the term "global village.")

There will be an increase of relays through satellite. India, for example, is negotiating for educational TV programing in schools to be relayed through stationary satellites, suspended over India. Perfected techniques may also make possible the direct transmissions of TV programs through satellite to receiver, in addition to ground station relay. This, in effect, will give TV transmission the present standing of direct shortwave broadcasts, with possible access to the sets of millions of people.

Cheaper mobile units with the use of videotape cameras will bring TV within the financial range of local authorities in the Third World who would otherwise wait for many years. Negotiations for mobile units in some nations are moving much more rapidly than the Christian public realizes.

And, pending new breakthroughs yet unknown, EVR (electronics video recordings) will provide TV receiver owners and educational authorities with small cartridges, very similar to tape recorder cartridges, which will contain one hour of sound film for use with an attachment to a TV set. By the mid-'70s many TV sets will contain a built-in cartridge holder as an integral part of the purchase.

EVR is already developed in black and white, and will be used in Britain in the '70s. Economical EVR color is only a few years away. The cost of production is very much lower than standard film. Major book publishers will offer EVR cartridges to supplement educational textbooks and in due course libraries will carry EVR cartridges as they now do books. The visual moving image will be as accessible and important as the printed page.

Christian planners need to take a long-term view early in the '70s and work well ahead of contemporary developments. It takes years to train skillful producers of first-class TV programs. Non-Christian technicians can be hired, but the production, writing of scripts, and communication of Christian ideas and the Good News for the Third World through TV call for national Christians committed to this specialized ministry.

Film production is inextricably linked with TV as a medium for communicating the gospel. Unfortunately, because of the taboo placed on movie theaters by some evangelicals, there is a paucity of Christian film producers. Many Christian colleges and Bible schools require their students to sign a pledge not to attend a movie theater. Even missionaries in mature adulthood are required by some mission societies to sign similar agreements. Rather than applying to the movies the same principle of selectivity used for books, where the evil is rejected and the good received, the total industry has been condemned by the institutions demanding such a pledge. TV has altered matters considerably. With the invasion of film into the home, reputable producers such as Moody Science Films, World Wide Pictures, and others began to offer films for church and public viewing, and the Christian film industry burgeoned in the '60s. But nearly all films were Western in content and orientation.

The '70s offer wide scope for film production aimed at

the non-Christian general public, as well as TV viewers. TV and film represent an open door of great influence in the Third World. Sensitive producers and artists will need to work closely together to produce culturally acceptable films and TV programs with Christian content for Third World viewers.

Africa has not yet developed a film industry. In Japan and India, even with their film studios and great secular market there are very few meaningful Christian films. And in the Western world, Christian films are in many cases like Christian radio programs, filled with clichés, and slanted to preconditioned Christian viewers. South America is a vast market for films, but only a handful of Christian productions are available for screening.

In many Third World nations the movie theater is the popular social center of the town, even more than the sports stadiums. Peanut sellers, ice cream vendors, and a chattering mob of young people crowd at the doors, waiting for the flood to burst out from the last show. This is the city rendezvous. "I'll meet you at the Rex, 6:30 show!" is shouted from one cyclist to another in the morning rush hour to work. In the villages the traveling cinemas set up a six-foot cloth screen and charge a few cents to viewers who crowd to sit on the ground and gawk at the pictures for two and a half hours at a time.

In Senegal, a crowd of French-speaking Muslim high schoolers willingly crammed into a courtyard to view the few available Moody Science films with French sound track. They would come three nights a week all year round if there were a supply of films.

In Kinshasa, Congo, in late 1969, a modern air-conditioned complex of TV, radio, and film studios equipped with editing rooms and a film processing lab was opened. Both Protestant and Roman Catholic programmers use these facilities. Tragically, no first-class evangelical French-speaking producers were ready for this new open door. Failure to foresee the possibilities in this area of communication impaired the ability of missions to use its technology with full effectiveness.

The challenge of Christian TV and film production in the '70s requires the training of Christians by apprenticeship in secular employment and in secular film schools such as the ones in Europe and America. Educational opportunities in this field will be duplicated in major Third World regions as the industry grows.

In Asia, Hong Kong Baptist College has introduced imaginative courses on communications which will eventually include TV and film production.

A suggested list of courses in this area include:

Dramatic literature	Visual communication
Film production	Theories of film
Feature film	Television documentary
Dramatic writing	Functional film
Experimental film	History of film
Theory of the cinema	Screen education

The involvement of national Christians in the planning stage is crucial if they are to participate in actual production and development. Otherwise a number of enthusiasts with money and technical know-how will enter the communications field and discover they have to fall back on Western canned programming because there are inadequate local Christian resources.

In today's secular world, creative ideas and local know-how are recognized as sources of financial wealth. The inventor of the long-playing record got a financier to back the patented process and received shares for his ideas. In twenty years he had become wealthy. Cannot the Christian financiers of the West who work for their Lord as trustees recognize the valid contribution of spiritual national artists and distributors and accord them equal rights in ownership and control? If this is done in the secular world, why should Christians of the Third World continue to remain employees instead of senior partners and shareholders in a consortium? By granting recognition to capable men, Christians of the affluent West can have the privilege and honor of partnership with their colleagues of the Third World in building and operating communication centers of great influence and importance in the work of Jesus Christ. They must establish Christian communications consortiums in which over 51 percent control will be invested in national Christian leadership who will have the authority and responsibility to finance and staff the TV and film programming.

Radio attracted financial investments totaling millions of dollars in the '50s and '60s. A network of Christian stations and bought-time facilities now beams Christian programs to every continent. Intermingling with the BBC, Radio Moscow, the Voice of Peking from Albania, and the Voice of America, the message of the gospel can be heard by millions in their mother tongue. Improved techniques will facilitate shortwave broadcasts and improve reception. Whatever else develops in the '70s, this medium will not be displaced.

Evangelism by radio to the Third World requires the musician, the artist, the writer, and the national evangelist, each specially skilled in the art of radio communication. The speaker, the participants in panel discussion, debate, play, or interview, must command attention to what is said by its relevance to local listeners' needs.

The words from Isaiah rang with new meaning as the Carpenter of Nazareth read them in the synagogue at a Sabbath worship. The same words have special meaning in the Third World: "the good news to the poor . . . liberty to captives and to the blind new sight, to set the downtrodden free" (Luke 4:18, Jerusalem Bible).

One of the programs in Hindi which drew the most listener response in India was prepared by an experienced missionary, Mr. Paul Schoonmaker, born in the country, fluent in Hindi, and very well read in Hindu philosophy. However, it is questionable whether, with the exception of special visitors and the few foreigners who by gift and skill demonstrate their calling in this direction, any Western voice should be used in evangelism to the Third World by radio. The very best broadcasters are national Christians with the developed skill of radio communication.

In Buenos Aires, Argentina, Spanish Christian radio programs were taped in modern studios. The wide listening audience packed the downtown stadium on a Saturday evening in 1966 on the invitation of two or three announcements at the end of the broadcast. The whole program was directed and planned by Argentines, and the popular radio preacher Mr. Vangioni reaches a wide audience of Roman Catholics.

Literature has held the center of evangelical missionary interest in the communications media. Despite the development of radio and the emergence of TV and film, this will continue to attract missionary interest through the '70s.

Creative writing in the cultural milieu is a priority. Sensitive artists and poets, thoughtful writers and thinkers will express the tensions, conflicts, and longings of each nation in new ways. Khwaja Abbas wrote *Inquilab* (*Revolution*), a powerful novel which became a living monument to the Indian fight for independence in the '40s. In the chapter "Storm Breaks" he describes "passive resistance": "Dawn broke over Bombay and the women were still there, fresh and defiant after fourteen hours of squatting. . . . When the half hour struck after 4 P.M. the police officers lost their nerves. They gave a final warning that if the women did not disperse in five minutes, they would be obliged to order a *lathi* (batons or sticks) charge." The reader's pulsebeat quickens, he feels the "thwack" of the sticks, sees the blood, hears the girls' piercing screams. The book brings a glow of pride to any Indian.

Christian writers must be helped to write effectively in their mother tongue. Their books will stir non-Christian readers to respond to Jesus Christ Who can answer their deepest problems and to react against the evil and corruption that sucks their nation dry of vital strength. Writing that conveys the Good News in the religious and cultural setting of its readers must be given top priority. The millions of students in universities, the young couples struggling with the bare needs of feeding and housing themselves and their children, the peasants in debt to the moneylender at extortionate interest—all need literature in their mother tongue. Very little contemporary material is available, and Western translated books are inadequate.

Radio programs, film scripts, TV plays and dialogue are all going to need the pens and typewriters of national writers. The Western teacher can help in sharing Western skills with them, in inculcating in them the love of literature—literature which he will himself have to love and study. But writing is so bound up with the feelings of the soul that very few Westerners ever enter the inner shrine of Third World cultures.

Of those few in each nation who have engaged in the profession successfully, most have edited or written under pen names. Close identification with the culture is the key. In one sense therefore, Christian writing is peculiarly the expression of a deep love for Christ by the national artist who longs to share His Lord with others. The techniques of the West, the efficient organizational scaffolding can do little in this sphere except to help market the product, for artists are not the best salesmen.

The Christian bookshop has served the Christian community well by making good literature available. Translations of Western Christian books, Christian books written locally, expensive imported books are sold at a profit, but the '70s call for much more promotional activity in this area of communications.

"Pas un pas sans Bata" says the red and yellow ad in Francophone Africa, and barefoot Africans save up the money to walk into the neat little Bata store and emerge with a pair of shoes. Marketing techniques sell tea to India—where it grows—but where it had not been previously used. Education in the techniques of marketing and modern packaging is one vital contribution that Westerners can make.

Marketing programs must move beyond the Christian bookshop, frequented by very few non-Christians, to where the people are. Good books by national authors, in attractive covers, with a neutral publishing name, can be placed in secular stores and on library shelves to good advantage. It is essential that Christian books be sold, and read, alongside the local novels and textbooks.

Communications are costly, but only in terms of cash

outlay. Great numbers can be reached through communications for far less money than it would cost to support the tens of thousands of preachers who would be required to reach the same number of people. If Western Christian agencies would see the possibilities in partnership with national leaders in the development of consortiums, they could offer financial investment and personnel to establish film and production studios for motion pictures, radio, and television for each major region and larger nation.

The words of President Nixon as the three astronauts rocketed outwards on their historic Apollo 11 moon landing of July, 1969, are significant:

> In past ages, exploration was a lonely enterprise; but today the miracles of space travel are matched by the miracles of space communication; even across the vast lunar distance, television brings the moment of discovery into our homes and makes all of us participants.

The miracles of space communication are the challenging frontiers of the '70s.

chapter ten

Tentmakers

They all worked together, for their trade was tentmaking.
—Acts 18:3, JBP

I'M going out through SCAAP on assignment to Uganda,"
Jim Brown, a Canadian teacher, said as he talked to a
mission executive. Four months later he was housed
in Kampala and immersed in his new job as assistant to
the high school principal.

"We have many African friends already, and life is
extremely interesting," his wife wrote to friends back
home. "I somehow feel we could never have got in touch
with so many people as missionaries."

Professor Maxim Jones, a Canadian from Vancouver,
taught physics in a Japanese university for one year.
His wife and two children quickly adjusted to living in
Japanese style. Soon a stream of students and others
were visiting them at home. Friends of their children

who attended a local school spread the word of open house. Their natural, radiant Christian faith was much more readily accepted when neighbors knew the academic standing and respect in which Professor Jones stood with his university colleagues. On his way back to Canada he was invited to lecture in mainland China. His academic hosts were disarmed by his professional competence and the obvious fact that his faith was personal conviction, not just propaganda for which he was paid a salary.

Mr. and Mrs. John Crane run a Fiat import agency in a large city of Africa. Three young Africans stayed in their home as boarders while studying at the local university. Mr. Crane is in constant demand as a preacher at local churches and as a speaker at conferences. The comings and goings of local Christians and foreign visitors make their home a hub of activity, and they are loved by African Christians whom they serve with much humility. Their objective advice, through counsel sought from them by several mission executives, has had a very healthy effect on mission policies.

Mr. Darwin Terrance is a well digger, assisting agricultural projects where the paucity of water threatened locals with crop failure. After generations of living in constant struggle for survival because of lack of water and resultant poor crops, the sparkling steady gush of water changed the whole atmosphere. "The water man," as Mr. Terrance was affectionately called, was a welcome guest anywhere. His radiant Christian faith rubbed off on many. "If this is Christianity, I will not oppose it," said one chief. "If my sons want to become Christians there will be no objection from me," said another.

In a large city in Iran, two American volunteers, Tim Anderson and Mark Merriam, worked with a group of

Muslim students, teaching advanced English. The Christian concepts which are the warp and woof of English literature were naturally explained as part of the lesson. The majestic prose of the Bible was introduced from time to time. In after-study hours, real friendship developed in the students' homes, and informal conversation ranged over the many questions about God, the world, the hope of mankind, the afterlife. The spontaneous atmosphere in which these two Christian volunteers could speak was very different from the tension and defensiveness of a session shared with those viewed as professional salaried propagandists.

Many Christians in business, professional, and government employment are going to travel to overseas assignments in the '70s. Twenty years ago most of them would have applied to missionary societies. A number of factors account for the gradual change of interest. One is the proliferation of agencies that have entered the field of aid to the developing nations following their independence. Previously this had been almost entirely the monopoly of missions. Another factor has been the growing dissatisfaction with missionary societies and their overseas programs. The evaluation of missions by foreign students in Western universities—not always objective—has made a number of young people uneasy about identification with missions. The overall gain for the work of Christ is the distribution of many Christians in all strata of life throughout many professions.

Missionary societies may experience a decline in total staff, but, in fact, unless cataclysmic international events close off frontiers, the '70s will see a continuing flow of Christian technicians, agriculturalists, health and medical personnel, and consultants in every conceivable profession serving on long- or short-term assignments in Third World nations. Christians can play an important role in international agencies and United Nations related organizations such as the International Labor Organization (ILO), Food and Agriculture Organization (FAO), Education, Scientific and Cultural Organizations (UNESCO), World Health Organization (WHO), and International Development Association (IDA).

The short term Peace Corps (United States), CUSO (Canada) and similar agencies of other Western nations provide many people with experience of overseas life and service as Christians. Young volunteers have a special influence on persons in their own age group and younger in the villages or towns where they are located. The insatiable curiosity about life in other lands, new ideas, and a genuine friendliness make a short-term assignment of two or three years very rewarding. If a volunteer can make friends with young people, he or she will survive the frustration of an older generation suspicious of change and particularly of youthful foreigners!

There are, of course, inherent dangers and problems in taking the bold step of employment and witness in a strange culture, but this adds challenge at a period of life when idealism is running full tide. The rocks and shoals, however, ought to be looked at on the charts.

At an Indian university two young Christians became so fascinated with Hindu philosophy that they gradually drifted away from Christian fellowship altogether and lost their faith. One young girl discovered that her witness to a single man involved her emotionally. His apparent interest in her religion was interest in her. They were married. He never became a Christian. Five years later the marriage broke up, and she returned to her parents with two children and a broken heart.

These are but two of any of a number of dangers, but the possible good that can result from answering the call to Christian commitment far outweighs the risk involved.

In the first century the Christian faith was rapidly spread by men and women in their normal pursuits of life. This is the mainstream of witness to the non-Christian world. National Christians are greatly encouraged and strengthened to witness for Christ by the vitality of Christian life that they observe in foreign business and professional men and women.

A nurse in a large Indian hospital said,

"There was an Australian supervisor in our hospital. She was very strict on asepsis and drug control; but she always seemed to have time for people who needed her help. We all knew she was a Christian, and several times I would have slurred over such things as using the same needle on two patients like some girls did. But, I thought of the supervisor, and took the trouble to boil up a fresh one. When the girls sold drugs in the bazaar, I refused to join them, just because of our supervisor."

If the '60s were any guide, most churches welcome and respect godly "tentmakers." They are outside the power struggles and the emotionally charged tensions stirring the churches. The host church soon gets to know the public reaction to a visitor through word-of-mouth reporting and insights of neighbors. A person is quickly classified and categorized: "A worldly fellow." "Loves his beer." "After women all the time." Or, "A hard worker." "An expert." "He prays in the morning before work and reads God's book."

The continuing tension between the European Marxist and the Western world eased in the '60s for business to develop on a wide scale. At Kiev airport, a British businessman explained carefully to a fellow traveler the long process involved in netting an order.

"Is it worth all this trouble?" the traveler inquired.

"My dear man, I wouldn't be here if it wasn't. The order will be worth about $3,000,000, so if I take a year to get it, what does it matter?"

Christian businessmen have carried their faith to many cities of Eastern Europe, and some have witnessed to top officials.

Trade links between mainland China and the Western world are likely to open in the '70s. Buying and selling will resume and international travel will include China on global air routes. Tourists will begin to reappear. Teachers of English will probably find job openings before the end of this decade. The tentmakers could be the first trickle of outside witnesses to reestablish contact not just with their business counterparts but with the churches also. An alertness to international developments will enable them to slip unobtrusively through any chink in the door to work for the Master. But because no publicity can be given to many tentmaking operations, prayer groups and churches in the Western world are especially obligated to pray for their members who follow this difficult approach in the tradition of some famous first century Christians.

Aquila and Priscilla were tentmakers. Refugees from Rome, they set up shop in the marketplace of Corinth. Their home provided Paul with his first base of operation in the city. They later traveled to Ephesus, and their home became a center for the Ephesian church. The last picture we have of them is back in Rome, and again a church is in their house; all the churches of the Gentiles are thankful to them for their partnership with Paul as fellow-workers (Acts 18:2–3, 18:18–19; 1 Corinthians 16:19 and Romans 16:3–5).

chapter eleven

Fellow Servants: 1976

THE quiet cool hiss of the air conditioner was broken by Mr. Wong's voice:

"Then we agree that as of January 31, 1976, our co-operating agencies and societies will operate in this sector of Asia under the name 'Consortium for Christian Communication in East Asia.'" He quickly glanced round the long oblong table at the men who had traveled from Europe, North America, and Australia for this historic conference with Asian Christian leaders.

"My people still have a problem, Mr. Wong," Paul Beckatof addressed the chairman. "What safeguards are there against an undue influence being exerted by any one cooperating group?"

"I think the protocol we signed was clear, Mr. Beckatof. We Asians will maintain 65 percent voting control. In the personnel committee we will decide the kind of persons we want, and we will advise your boards accordingly. We shall be careful to absorb new personnel on the agreed percentage basis from each group, all other qualifications being equal."

"How will you be sure they are committed to historic Christianity?" asked Mr. Chou.

"Let's ask our personnel officer to answer," Mr. Wong nodded to Mr. Sanvido of Manila.

"As you know, brothers, there is a statement of faith. We have photocopies of accepted candidate forms, and then there is the six months probation period on arrival." Sanvido coughed, then sipped at his green tea and went on.

"The three interviews arranged with our personnel committee reveal quite a lot. We will watch the new arrival."

"What about the case of Smith?" Beckatof broke in, pressing his large hands under the table.

"That's the very point, Brother Beckatof. During the probationary period we found out that he accepted the story of the resurrection as a myth with a spiritual meaning, but not as historical fact. There was no alternative; we asked his board to withdraw him."

"I know, I know. His church wasn't very happy, and they refused to put the consortium on their budget."

"One other matter please," Mr. Sidjabat of Indonesia had the floor. "This matter of our liberty to fraternize with all whom we regard as true Christian brethren— does this clause guarantee no further interference by our Western brothers in our decisions?"

Mr. Wong nodded again to Mr. Sanvido. "It has taken a long time to persuade our Western brothers to trust us," Mr. Sanvido said, "but after the Henning incident it is clear. You remember that Henning's board insisted he withdraw permission for the broadcasts of our Episcopal friend from India, because of their supporters' pressure?" There was a moving of chairs, and a rustle round the table. Mr. Sanvido again sipped his tea.

"When we told Henning that this was foreign interference, and he had to decide between partnership with us in Asia, or obedience to his home board, well, you know, he deferred to the board. It brought the issue into the open and we now have clause 16C which protects the consortium from such incidents in the future."

"I move we approve the amendments. We have been three days at this, and our home boards have given due consideration to all possible implications."

"I second Mr. Richmond," Mr. Chou lifted his hand.

Outside the tenth-story window, the neon lights threw their rosy glow on the ships bobbing at anchor opposite Kowloon. The faint whine of a climbing jumbo jetliner penetrated the walls. The hands on Mr. Wong's watch pointed to midnight. The 1976 consortium development had taken five years to negotiate, but now the upraised hands of the men around the table gave Mr. Wong a sense of relaxed ease. Soon he would move towards the ferry and home, and in his heart he rejoiced to know that a great new day for the gospel had dawned.

Mr. Wong had served very humbly as chairman of the negotiating committee to establish a new basis of management and direction for a number of institutions in Southeast Asia. The literature groups had been relatively easy to deal with, especially the editorial centers. There were still so few gifted Christian writers that the nineteen societies involved were only too glad to cooperate. The radio stations had been more difficult, especially when the foreign broadcasters discovered that their tapes were no longer in demand, or even needed.

"But my one million listeners back home give substantial sums," one popular programmer had protested.

"It's not only a matter of money, but of what is best for our people," Mr. Wong had replied very gently.

"But the gospel is what the people need. It's the one answer to Communism. After South Vietnam . . . surely you've learned that lesson," the Western programmer had argued.

Mr. Wong had poured his guest some more tea. "You remember Mr. Lee?" he had asked.

"That man! Why, sure, as good a Chinese brother as I know."

"Would you like to think Mr. Lee is giving the gospel to his own people, Mr. Wainwright?" The long silence had won assent.

The new film units were budgeting for such large sums that no one group could possibly have raised the money alone. The producers found it difficult not to have a completely free hand, but they had learned that local culture must be respected, especially after the bacon and eggs incident. Mr. Wong's normally placid face creased into a smile as he remembered the Malaysian reaction to seeing a scene where a Muslim was eating bacon and eggs for breakfast. Well, it had been caught in time. They had five national producers now, none of whom were likely to repeat that mistake.

God had helped them. Surely the blessing was because of the unity which had grown over the years, and now many spiritual young people were applying for staff positions.

Mr. Wong snapped out of his reverie and quickened his step. This was very late to get home, very late indeed.

* * *

Ted Hill watched the snowflakes drift down past the window. He was glad the rapid transit turbo train to

Boston had replaced the old air shuttle out of La Guardia. If this lasted all day, things would really be fouled up on the roads. Maybe he would get home on the 7:00 P.M. train.

"Ted, can we have the reaction of your board to the position paper?" Bob Johnson's question pulled Ted back into the room where the twenty-one men were meeting.

"We are prepared to go along with this, but we do not feel we can drop our home image."

"What do you mean?" queried Bob.

"I guess we're all in the same situation. Our home constituency gives to, prays for, thinks of *our* work. They'll find it difficult to adjust to combined operations for some time. We'll have to keep on the magazine. We can't merge the home operations yet, only the field."

"Let's take the first step on the field, right?" broke in Dan Butler.

"We release our best missionary staff, men and women, to the combined evangelistic teaching teams and to the united training and research centers. Those in communications go to the new consortium."

Ted Hill leaned forward. "Are we really prepared for the control to be in the hands of the national teams?"

"That's the whole idea, isn't it?" said Dan. "Phase out the old, phase in the new."

"But what about the money, fellows? It's our money. They want to control our money!" a voice said from the end of the table.

"Is it our money? Where did it come from?" Bob Johnson rapped the table.

"Well, sure! The churches, the individual supporters gave to *our* missions."

"Did they really give it to *us* or to *God?*" Ted Hill

broke in. "Look. Let's get this straight. When money is given to God it is neutralized. Why shouldn't the Asian teams be just as good trustees as ourselves? You are talking like a businessman, not as a servant of God." Ted pushed back his chair.

"What's the alternative to cooperation under their leadership?" Dan asked. "We can't last another five years. Soon there won't be a field left in Asia that will tolerate the old pattern of white missionary programing."

"Brethren," Gustafson spoke up. "In Norway we think differently. My friends here," and he nodded to his Finnish and Swedish colleagues, "agreed last night when we talked until late about our attitude. We want to work with our Asian brothers on their teams. In fact, we've been doing this for several years. Let's try this. There's no other way now; it's too late. This is 1976. I vote for the positive now."

"Second," said Dan.

Murmured assent, raised hands, and the decision was made to offer personnel and substantial financial pledges to the Asian team's operation, the training and research centers, and the consortiums which were operating on an interim basis. Such an event marked an historic turning point in the history of some twenty-five European, Commonwealth, and American missionary societies. Similar consultations were planned for Africa and South America following the basic change in policies by a number of progressive Western missionary societies.

From then on new personnel was absorbed on an apprenticeship basis in the team ministries of twenty-five nations of Asia. Teachers followed the evangelists in a planned six-month teaching course. Western mission-

aries were always an unobtrusive minority. Experienced and specially gifted men and women now were no longer called missionaries, but evangelists, teachers, advisers, or consultants. They worked alongside national colleagues who directed the programs. In the follow-up work, Westerners were assigned to work with Asians to introduce them to the ministry of expounding Scripture —opening up the Bible by the inductive method of teaching—and the application of Bible truth to local situations.

Halfway through the course, the roles were switched, and national colleagues took over, with the counsel of the Western teacher given daily for the remaining quarter. In the final quarter, the Western adviser gave advice only when asked, but in each class he made notes and at the end gave a summarized suggestion and evaluation paper to his partner.

During the last quarter he spent time in personal counseling with leaders, preparation for the next course, and writing. Very little tension was expected. The national colleague knew he would be on his own later. This was the last time a Western consultant would be assigned to work with him and he wanted to learn as much as he could.

Western teachers and evangelists assigned to regional work chose their own place of residence, generally in the suburbs of megapolises such as Singapore, Manila, Tokyo, or Hong Kong. Some married couples with teenage children maintained their residences in their country of origin, living in Melbourne, Vancouver, San Francisco, Hamburg, Oslo, and working in three-month cycles. Airbus transportation made it cheaper for the man to travel while his children attended free school at home than for him to bring out the whole family and pay for schooling. But each of these men living at home base had served five or more years of apprenticeship in one or another of the cultures of the region, had learned one language well, and was oriented to Asia. Their travel budget was approved by the regional teams committees, and the annual cycle of ministry also.

Men and women working in national team ministries lived in convenient centers near main transportation facilities in the nations of their ministry (such as Tokyo in Japan, Santiago for Chile, or Kinshasa for the Congo). They spent two years in intensive language study and orientation to a secular environment. They were expected to absorb as much as possible of the local and contemporary viewpoint. As evangelists and teachers— or as Paul had written, 'ambassadors'—they had to know empathetically the people whom they had been called to serve. As a result they had many local friends and served a number of churches.

Ted Hill settled into his turbo transit chair as it pressed into his back with rapid acceleration towards Boston and home. Tension had ebbed, leaving him bone-weary.

There is something to be said for our role as advisers, he thought. Asian Christians will carry the responsibility now; but as servants of God, and co-laborers with them, I guess we'll work just as hard as ever to back them up.

Notes

Chapter 1

1. Leonard Bertin, *Target 2067* (Macmillan of Canada).
2. Pierre Teilhard de Chardin, *The Future of Man* (New York: Harper and Row, 1964).

Chapter 2

1. 13,575 related to member agencies of the interdenominational Foreign Missions Association and Evangelical Foreign Missions Association and 8,406 others. *N. American Protestant Ministries Overseas* (New York: Missionary Research Library, 1968).

Chapter 3

1. Kenneth S. Latourette, *A History of Christianity* (New York: Harper and Bros., 1953).
2. *A Study of the Older Protestant Missions and Churches in Peru and Chile*, Oosterbaan and Le Cointre N. V. (Goes, 1967), pp. 127, 130.
3. David Barrett, *Schism and Renewal in Africa* (New York: Oxford University Press, 1968).